AF516297

*Viva Modern Critical Interpretations*

# William Shakespeare's Othello

## *Bloom's Modern Critical Interpretations*

Adventures of Huckleberry Finn
All Quiet on the Western Front
Animal Farm
Beloved
Beowulf
Billy Budd, Benito Cereno, Bartleby the Scrivener, and Other Tales
The Bluest Eye
Brave New World
Cat on a Hot Tin Roof
The Catcher in the Rye
Catch-22
Cat's Cradle
The Color Purple
Crime and Punishment
The Crucible
Daisy Miller, The Turn of the Screw, and Other Tales
David Copperfield
Death of a Salesman
The Divine Comedy
Don Quixote
Dracula
Dubliners
Emma
Fahrenheit 451
A Farewell to Arms
Frankenstein
The General Prologue to the Canterbury Tales
The Glass Menagerie
The Grapes of Wrath
Great Expectations
The Great Gatsby
Gulliver's Travels
Hamlet
The Handmaid's Tale
Heart of Darkness
I Know Why the Caged Bird Sings
The Iliad
The Interpretation of Dreams
Invisible Man
Jane Eyre
The Joy Luck Club
Julius Caesar
The Jungle
King Lear
Long Day's Journey Into Night
Lord of the Flies
The Lord of the Rings
Macbeth
The Merchant of Venice
The Metamorphosis
A Midsummer Night's Dream
Moby-Dick
My Ántonia
Native Son
Night
1984
The Odyssey
Oedipus Rex
The Old Man and the Sea
One Flew Over the Cuckoo's Nest
One Hundred Years of Solitude
Othello
Paradise Lost
The Pardoner's Tale
A Portrait of the Artist as a Young Man
Pride and Prejudice
Ragtime
The Red Badge of Courage
The Rime of the Ancient Mariner
Romeo & Juliet
The Scarlet Letter
A Scholarly Look at The Diary of Anne Frank
A Separate Peace
Silas Marner
Slaughterhouse-Five
Song of Myself
Song of Solomon
The Sonnets of William Shakespeare
Sophie's Choice
The Sound and the Fury
The Stranger
A Streetcar Named Desire
Sula
The Sun Also Rises
A Tale of Two Cities
The Tales of Poe
The Tempest
Tess of the D'Urbervilles
Their Eyes Were Watching God
Things Fall Apart
To Kill a Mockingbird
Waiting for Godot
Walden
The Waste Land
White Noise
Wuthering Heights

VIVA MODERN CRITICAL INTERPRETATIONS

# William Shakespeare's
# OTHELLO

*Edited and with an Introduction by*

**HAROLD BLOOM**

**Sterling Professor of the Humanities**
**Yale University**

**Viva Books Private Limited**

New Delhi • Mumbai • Chennai • Kolkata • Bangalore • Hyderabad

First Indian Edition 2007

**VIVA BOOKS PRIVATE LIMITED**

- 4737/23 Ansari Road, Daryaganj, New Delhi 110 002
E-mail: vivadelhi@vivagroupindia.net, Tel. 42242200
- Plot No. 76, Service Industries, Shirvane, Sector 1, Nerul, Navi Mumbai 400 706
E-mail: vivamumbai@vivagroupindia.net, Tel. 27721273, 27721274
- Jamals Fazal Chambers, 26 Greams Road, Chennai 600 006
E-mail: vivachennai@vivagroupindia.net, Tel. 28290304, 28294241
- B-103, Jindal Towers, 21/1A/3 Darga Road, Kolkata 700 017
E-mail: vivakolkata@vivagroupindia.net, Tel. 22836381, 22816713
- 7, Sovereign Park Apartments, 56-58, K. R. Road, Basavanagudi, Bangalore 560 004
E-mail: vivabangalore@vivagroupindia.net, Tel.26607409, 26607410
- 101-102 Mughal Marc Apartments, 3-4-637 to 641, Narayanguda, Hyderabad 500 029
E-mail: vivahyderabad@vivagroupindia.net, Tel. 27564481, 27564482

*Published by arrangement with*

Facts on File, Inc.
132 West 31st Street
New York NY 10001
USA



All links and web addresses were checked and verified to be correct at the time of publication. Because of the dynamic nature of the web, some addresses and links may have changed since publication and may no longer be valid.

Every effort been made to trace the owners of copyrighted material and secure copyight permission. Articles appearing in this volume generally appear much as they did in their original publication with little to no editorial changes. Those interested in locating the original source will find bibliographic information on the first page of each article as well as in the bibliography and acknowledgments sections of this volume.



ISBN 81-309-0698-8

Published by Vinod Vasishtha for Viva Books Private Limited, 4737/23 Ansari Road
New Delhi-110 002. Printed and bound at Anand Sons, Delhi-110 092.

# Contents

# Editor's Note

This book brings together what I judge to be a representative selection of the best modern criticism on Shakespeare's tragedy *Othello*. The critical essays are reprinted here in the chronological sequence of their original publication. I am grateful to Cornelia Pearsall for her aid in editing this volume.

My introduction meditates upon Iago as an incarnate spirit of war, following a suggestion of Harold Goddard. The chronological sequence of criticism begins with the philosopher Stanley Cavell, who develops his insight that "Iago is everything Othello must deny, and which, denied, is not killed but works on, like poison, like furies."

Susan Snyder emphasizes a tension in *Othello* between general and particular senses of "nature," so as to indicate Shakespeare's apprehension of "the vulnerability of love." In an analysis of power in the play, Stephen Greenblatt broods on what he calls "an *excessive* aesthetic delight," the love of Desdemona for Othello, which intimates a power more profoundly subversive than any power manifested either by Othello or Iago.

Mark Rose reads the play as Othello's "martial pastoral," a belated romance of chivalry subjected to the tortures of Iago's experimentalism. Studying love, sexuality, and marriage in *Othello*, Carol Thomas Neely finds no resolutions in "the pain and derision of the ending," in which "the conflict between the men and the women has not been eliminated or resolved."

Patricia Parker, in an advanced rhetorical reading, reminds us that Shakespeare's language needs to be heard on every level of discourse in which Renaissance rhetoric is embedded: politics, theology, logic, the ideology of sexual difference. In a general overview of *Othello*, the distinguished poet Anthony Hecht, whose own poetry is deeply tinged by

Shakespeare's Venetian tragedy, finds "a painful but undoubted nobility" in Othello's suicide, which has caused considerable controversy in modern criticism.

# Introduction

## I

Dr. Samuel Johnson found in the representation of Othello, Iago, and Desdemona "such proofs of Shakespeare's skill in human nature, as, I suppose, it is vain to seek in any modern writer." The High Romantic Victor Hugo gave us the contrary formula: "Next to God, Shakespeare created most," which does not seem to me a remystification of Shakespeare's characters, but rather a shrewd hint in what might be called the pragmatics of aesthetics. Shakespeare was a mortal god (as Hugo aspired to be) because his art was not a mimesis at all. A mode of representation that is always out ahead of any historically unfolding reality necessarily contains us more than we can contain it. A. D. Nuttall wonderfully remarks of Iago that he "chooses which emotions he will experience. He is not just motivated, like other people. Instead he *decides* to be motivated." Though Nuttall says that makes of Iago a Camus-like existentialist, I would think Iago is closer to a god, or a devil, and so perhaps resembles his creator, who evidently chose emotions to be experienced, and decided whether or not to be motivated. We do not feel Othello to be a critique of Shakespeare, but in some sense Iago is just that, being a playwright, like Edmund in *King Lear*, like Hamlet, and like William Shakespeare. Hamlet's "the rest is silence" has a curious parallel in Iago's "from this time forth I never will speak word," even though Hamlet dies immediately and Iago survives to die mutely under torture.

It is not that Iago is in Hamlet's class as an intellectual consciousness. No, Iago is comparable to Edmund, who in *King Lear* out-plots everyone else in the royal world of the play. Othello is a glorious soldier and a sadly simple man, who could have been ruined by a villain far less gifted than Iago. A. C. Bradley's charming notion is still true: exchange Othello and

Hamlet in one another's plays, and there would be no plays. Othello would chop Claudius down as soon as the ghost had convinced him, and Hamlet would have needed only a few moments to see through Iago, and to begin destroying him by overt parody. But there are no Hamlets, Falstaffs, or inspired clowns in *Othello, The Moor of Venice*, and poor Desdemona is no Portia.

*The Moor of Venice* is sometimes the neglected part of the tragedy's title. To be the Moor of Venice, its hired general, is an uneasy honor, Venice being, then and now, the uneasiest of cities. Othello's pigmentation is notoriously essential to the plot. He is hardly a natural man in relation to the subtle Venetians, but the sexual obsessiveness he catches from Iago develops into a dualism that renders him insane. A marvelous monism has yielded to the discontents of Venetian civilization, and we remain haunted by intimations of a different Othello, as though Desdemona, even before Iago's intervention, has been loss as well as gain for the previously integral soldier. Many critics have noted Othello's ruefulness when he speaks in act 1 of having exchanged his "unhoused free condition" for his love of "the gentle Desdemona." When we think of him in his glory we remember his ending a street battle with one line of marvelous authority:

> Keep up your bright swords, for the dew will rust them.

"Sheathe or die" would be the reductive reading, but Othello in his zenith defies reduction, and a fuller interpretation would emphasize the easiness and largeness of this superbly military temperament. How does so spacious and majestic an authority degenerate so rapidly into an equivalent of Spenser's Malbecco? Like Malbecco, Othello forgets he is a man and his name in effect becomes Jealousy. Jealousy in Hawthorne becomes Satan, after having been Chillingworth, while in Proust, first Swann and then Marcel become art historians of jealousy, as it were, obsessive scholars desperately searching for every visual detail of betrayal. Freud's *delusional* jealousy involves repressed homosexuality, and seems inapplicable to Othello, though not wholly so to Iago. Jealousy in Shakespeare—parent to its presence in Hawthorne, Proust, and Freud—is a mask for the fear of death, since what the jealous lover fears is that there will not be time or space enough for himself. It is one of the peculiar splendors of *Othello* that we cannot understand Othello's belated jealousy without first understanding Iago's primal envy of Othello, which is at the hidden center of the drama. drama.

## II

Frank Kermode curiously says that "Iago's naturalist ethic . . . is a wicked man's version of Montaigne," a judgment that Ben Jonson might have welcomed, but that I find alien to Shakespeare. Iago is not a naturalist but the fiercest version in all literature of an ideologue of the reductive fallacy, which can be defined as the belief that what is most real about any one of us is the worst thing that possibly could be true of us. "Tell me what she or he is *really* like," the reductionist keeps saying, and means: "Tell me the worst thing you can." Presumably the reductionist cannot bear to be deceived, and so becomes a professional at deception.

Iago is Othello's standard-bearer, a senior officer skilled and courageous in the field, as we have every reason to believe. "I am not what I am" is his chilling motto, and is endless to meditation. "I am that I am" is God's name in answer to the query of Moses, and reverberates darkly and antithetically in "I am not what I am." God will be where and when He will be, present or absent as is His choice. Iago is the spirit that will not be, the spirit of absence, a pure negativity. We know therefore from the start why Iago hates Othello, who is the largest presence, the fullest being in Iago's world, and particularly in battle. The hatred pretends to be empirical, but is ontological, and unquenchable in consequence. If Platonic eros is the desire for what one hasn't got, then Iago's hatred is the drive to destroy what one hasn't got. We shudder when the maddened Othello vows death to Desdemona as a "fair devil" and promotes Iago to be his lieutenant, for Iago superbly responds, "I am your own for ever," and means the reverse: "You too are now an absence."

Step by step, Iago falls into his own gap of being, changing as he hears himself plot, improvising a drama that must destroy the dramatist as well as his protagonists:

> IAGO: And what's he then that says I play the villain,
> When this advice is free I give, and honest,
> Probal to thinking, and indeed the course
> To win the Moor again? For 'tis most easy
> Th' inclining Desdemona to subdue
> In any honest suit; she's fram'd as fruitful
> As the free elements. And then for her
> To win the Moor, were['t] to renounce his baptism.
> All seals and symbols of redeemed sin,
> His soul is so enfetter'd to her love,

That she may make, unmake, do what she list,
Even as her appetite shall play the god
With his weak function. How am I then a villain,
To counsel Cassio to this parallel course,
Directly to his good? Divinity of hell!
When devils will the blackest sins put on,
They do suggest at first with heavenly shows,
As I do now; for whiles this honest fool
Plies Desdemona to repair his fortune,
And she for him pleads strongly to the Moor,
I'll pour this pestilence into his ear—
That she repeals him for her body's lust,
And by how much she strives to do him good,
She shall undo her credit with the Moor.
So will I turn her virtue into pitch,
And out of her own goodness make the net
That shall enmesh them all.

Harold C. Goddard called Iago a "moral pyromaniac," and we can hear Iago setting fire to himself throughout the play, but particularly in this speech. I think that Goddard, a profoundly imaginative critic, captured the essence of Iago when he saw that Iago was always at war, making every encounter, every moment, into an act of destruction. War is the ultimate reductive fallacy, since to kill your enemy you must believe the worst that can be believed about him. What changes in Iago as he listens to himself is that he loses perspective, because his rhetoric isolates by burning away context. Isolation, Freud tells us, is the compulsive's guarantee that the coherence of his thinking will be interrupted. Iago interposes intervals of monologue so as to defend himself against his own awareness of change in himself, and thus ironically intensifies his own change into the totally diabolic. As with Shakespeare's Richard III, Iago's monologues are swerves away from the Divine "I am that I am," past "I am not what I am," on to "I am not," negation mounting to an apotheosis.

The collapse of Othello is augmented in dignity and poignance when we gain our full awareness of Iago's achieved negativity, war everlasting. No critic need judge Othello to be stupid, for Othello does not incarnate war, being as he is a sane and honorable warrior. He is peculiarly vulnerable to Iago precisely because Iago is his standard-bearer, the protector of his colors and reputation in battle, pledged to die rather than allow the colors to be taken. His equivalent to Iago's monologues is a stirring elegy for the self, a farewell to war as a valid—because confined—occupation:

> OTHELLO: I had been happy, if the general camp,
> Pioners and all, had tasted her sweet body,
> So I had nothing known. O now, for ever
> Farewell the tranquil mind! farewell content!
> Farewell the plumed troops and the big wars
> That makes ambition virtue! O, farewell!
> Farewell the neighing steed and the shrill trump,
> The spirit-stirring drum, th' ear-piercing fife,
> The royal banner, and all quality,
> Pride, pomp, and circumstance of glorious war!
> And O you mortal engines, whose rude throats
> Th' immortal Jove's dread clamors counterfeit,
> Farewell! Othello's occupation's gone.

"Pride, pomp, and circumstance of glorious war!" has yielded to Iago's incessant war against being. Othello, within his occupation's limits, has the greatness of the tragic hero. Iago breaks down those limits from within, from war's own camp, and so Othello has no chance. Had the attack come from the world outside war's dominion, Othello could have maintained some coherence, and gone down in the name of the purity of arms. Shakespeare, courting a poetics of pain, could not allow his hero that consolation.

# Epistemology and Tragedy:
## A Reading of *Othello*

*Stanley Cavell*

The last part of the book of which my reading of *Othello* takes the last pages is in effect a meditation on the relation between the title concepts of the two concluding essays of my book *Must We Mean What We Say?*—"Knowing and Acknowledging" and "The Avoidance of Love: A Reading of *King Lear*"—that is, a meditation on the reciprocity between acknowledgment and avoidance, hence between skepticism and tragedy. In particular, the reading of *Othello* is the most detailed of several moments I choose in Shakespeare from which to study the imagination of the body's fate in the progress of skepticism.

To orient ourselves, let us begin by considering briefly how it is that we are to understand, at the height of *The Winter's Tale*, Hermione's reappearance as a statue. Specifically I ask how it is that we are to understand Leontes's acceptance of the "magic" that returns her to flesh and blood, and hence to him. This is a most specific form of resurrection. Accepting it means accepting the idea that she had been turned to stone; that that was the right means for her disappearance from life. So I am asking for the source of Leontes's conviction in the rightness of that fate. Giving the question that form, the form of my answer is by now predictable: for her to return to him is for him to acknowledge her; and for him to acknowledge her is for him to acknowledge his relation to her; in particular to acknowledge what his denial of her has done to her, hence to him. So Leontes recognizes the fate of stone to be the consequence of his particular

From *Hypocrisy, Illusion and Evasion*, *Daedalus* 108, no. 3 (Summer 1979). 

skepticism. One can see this as the projection of his own sense of numbness, of living death. But then why was this *his* fate? It is a most specific form of remorse or of (self-) punishment.

Its environment is provided by a tale of harrowing by jealousy, and a consequent accusation of adultery—an accusation known by everyone else to be insanely false. Hence Leontes is inevitably paired with Othello. I call attention to two further ways in which *The Winter's Tale* is a commentary on *Othello*, and therefore contrariwise. First, both plays involve a harrowing of the power of knowing the existence of another (as chaste, intact, as what the knower knows his other to be). Leontes refuses to believe a true oracle; Othello insists on believing a false one. Second, in both plays the consequence for the man's refusal of knowledge of his other is an imagination of stone. It is not merely an appetite for beauty that produces Othello's most famous image of his victim as a piece of cold and carved marble ("whiter skin of hers than snow, / And smooth, as monumental alabaster"). Where does his image come from?

Before I can give my answer I still need one further piece of orientation in thinking of tragedy as a kind of epistemological problem, or as the outcome of the problem of knowledge—of the dominance of modern philosophical thought by the problem of knowledge. Earlier, in meditating on the existence of other minds, I was led to ask how we are to understand the other as having displaced or absorbed the weight of God, the task of showing me that I am not alone in the universe. I was claiming there to be giving a certain derivation for the problem of the other. But I was also echoing one formulation Descartes gives his motive in wanting to find what is beyond doubt, namely, to know beyond doubt that he is not alone in the world (Third Meditation). Now I ask, in passing but explicitly, why is it Descartes does not try to defeat that possibility of isolation in what would seem the directest and surest way, by locating the existence of one other finite being.

He says simply that he can easily imagine that ideas "which represent men similar to myself" could be "formed by the combination of my other ideas, of myself, of corporeal objects, and of God, even though outside of me there were no other men in the world." He is, of course, setting up a powerful move toward God. And we can gather from this—something that seems borne out in the sequel of this piece of writing—that the problem of others (other finite beings) is not discovered, or derived, by Descartes to be a special problem of knowledge; this is surely one reason it would not have been discovered to be such in subsequent epistemology. However, the more one meditates on the unique place Descartes makes for his relation to his own body, the less clear and distinct it is that he has available to himself the formulation of the idea of another body as having a unique relation to its mind, in that special quasisubstantial way that he asserts is not like the way a ship is related to its pilot. But without such an idea, what is the content of the idea of "men similar to myself"? I do not conceive of Descartes's appealing to the route of analogy here, since he must be far surer that other human bodies go with minds than any sureness he can extract by inferring from another body's behavior alone. After all, the body has essentially nothing to do with the soul! In the light of this passing of the question of the other, a change is noticeable in the coda Descartes supplies his argument at the end of this third meditation:

> The whole force of the argument I have here used to prove the existence of God consists in the fact that I recognize that it would not be possible for my nature to be what it is, possessing the idea of a God, unless God really existed—the same God, I say, the idea of whom I possess, the God who possesses all these high perfections . . . [who] cannot be a deceiver.

The main point of summary is that I could not have produced the idea I have of God, for it can have come from nothing less than God himself. But a new note of necessity is also struck, that without the presence of this idea in myself, and (hence) the presence of the fact of which it is the imprint, my own nature would necessarily not be what it is. So not only the fact, as it were, of my existence, but the integrity of it, depends on this idea. (And so these meditations are about the finding of self-knowledge after all; of the knowledge of a human self by a human self.)

That the integrity of my (human, finite) existence may depend on the fact and on the idea of another being's existence, and on the possibility of *proving* that existence—an existence conceived from my very dependence and incompleteness, hence conceived as perfect, and conceived as producing me "in some sense, in [its] own image"—these are thoughts that take me to a study of *Othello*.

Briefly, to begin with, we have the logic, the emotion, and the scene of skepticism epitomized. The logic: "My life upon her faith" (1.3.295) [All *Othello* citations are to *Complete Works of Shakespeare*, ed. G. B. Harrison] and "when I love thee not / Chaos is come again" (3.3.91–92) set up the stake necessary to best cases; the sense I expressed by the imaginary major premise, "If I know anything, I know this." One standing issue about the rhythm of *Othello*'s plot is that the progress from the completeness of Othello's love to the perfection of his doubt is too precipitous for the fictional time of the play. But such precipitousness is just the rhythm of skepticism; all that is necessary is the stake. The emotion: Here I mean not exactly Othello's emotion toward Desdemona, call it jealousy; but rather the structure of his emotion as he is hauled back and forth across the keel of his love. Othello's enactment, or sufferance, of that torture is the most extraordinary representation known to me of the "astonishment" in skeptical doubt. In the First Meditation we read: "I realize so clearly that there are no conclusive indications by which waking life can be distinguished from sleep that I am quite astonished, and my bewilderment is such that it is almost able to convince me that I am sleeping." (It does not follow that one is *convinced* that one is awake.) When Othello loses consciousness ("Is 't possible?—Confess?—Handkerchief?—Oh, devil!" [4.1.43–44]), it is not from conviction in a piece of knowledge but in an effort to stave the knowledge off. The scene: Here I have in mind the pervasive air of the language and the action of this play as one in which Othello's mind continuously outstrips reality, dissolves it in trance or dream or in the beauty or ugliness of his incantatory imagination; in which he visualizes possibilities that reason, unaided, cannot rule out. Why is he beyond aid? Why are the ear and the eye in him disjoined? We know that by the time he formulates his condition this way:

> By the world,
> I think my wife be honest, and think she is not.
> I think that thou art just, and think thou art not.
> I'll have some proof
>
> (3.3.383–86)

he is lost. Two dozen lines earlier he had demanded of Iago "the ocular proof," a demand which was no purer a threat than it was a command, as if he does indeed wish for this outcome, as if he has a use for Iago's suspicions, hence a use for Iago that reciprocates Iago's use of him. Nothing I claim about the play here will depend on an understanding of the relation between Iago and Othello, so I will simply assert what is suggested by what I have just said, that such a question as "Why does Othello believe Iago?" is badly formed. It is not conceivable that Othello believes Iago and *not* Desdemona. Iago, we might say, offers Othello an opportunity to believe something, something to oppose to something else he knows. What does he know? Why does it require opposition? What do we know?

We have known (say since G. Wilson Knight's "The Othello Music") that Othello's language, call it his imagination, is at once his and the play's glory, and his shame; the source of his power and of his impotence; or we should have known (since Bradley's *Shakespearean Tragedy*) that Othello is the most romantic of Shakespeare's heroes, which may be a way of summarizing the same facts. And we ought to attend to the perception that Othello is the most Christian of the tragic heroes (expressed in Norman Rabkin's *Shakespeare and the Common Understanding*). Nor is there any longer any argument against our knowledge that Othello is black; and there can be no argument with the fact that he has just married, nor with the description, compared with the case of Shakespeare's other tragedies, that this one is not political but domestic.

We know more specifically, I take it, that Othello's blackness means something. But what specifically does it mean? Mean, I mean, to him—for otherwise it is not Othello's color that we are interested in but some generalized blackness, meaning perhaps "sooty" or "filthy," as elsewhere in the play. This difference may show in the way one takes Desdemona's early statement: "I saw Othello's visage in his mind" (1.3.253). I think it is commonly felt that she means she overlooked his blackness in favor of his inner brilliance; and perhaps further felt that this is a piece of deception, at least of herself. But what the line more naturally says is that she saw his visage as he sees it, that she understands his blackness as he understands it, as the expression (or in his word, his manifestation) of his mind—which is not overlooking it. Then how does he understand it?

As the color of a romantic hero. For he, as he was and is, manifested by his parts, his title, and his "perfect soul" (1.2.31), is the hero of the tales of romance he tells, some ones of which he wooed and won Desdemona with, others of which he will die upon. It is accordingly the color of one with enchanted powers and magical protection, but above all it is the color of one of purity, of a perfect soul. Desdemona, in entering his life, hence in entering his story of his life, enters as a fit companion for such a hero; his perfection is now opened toward hers. His absolute stake in his purity, and its confirmation in hers, is shown in what he feels he has lost in losing Desdemona's confirmation:

> My name, that was as fresh
> As Dian's visage, is now begrimed and black
> As mine own face.
>
> (3.3.386–88)

Diana's is a name for the visage Desdemona saw to be in Othello's mind. He loses its application to his own name, his charmed self, when he no longer sees his visage in Desdemona's mind but in Iago's, say in the world's capacity for rumor. To say he loses Desdemona's power to confirm his image of himself is to say that he loses his old power of imagination. And this is to say that he loses his grasp of his own nature; he no longer has the same voice in his history. So then the question becomes: How has he come to displace Desdemona's imagination with Iago's? However terrible the exchange, it must be less terrible than some other. Then we need to ask not so much how Iago gained his power as how Desdemona lost hers.

We know, one gathers, that Desdemona has lost her virginity, the protection of Diana, by the time she appears to us. And surely Othello knows this! But this change in her condition, while a big enough fact to hatch millennia of plots, is not what Othello accuses her of. (Though would that accusation have been much more unfair than the unfaithfulness he does accuse her of?) I emphasize that I am assuming that in Othello's mind the theme and condition of virginity carry their full weight within a romantic universe. Here is Northrop Frye, writing on the subject recently: "Deep within the stock convention of virgin-baiting is a vision of human integrity imprisoned in a world it is in but not of, often forced by weakness into all kinds of ruses and strategems, yet always managing to avoid the one fate which really is worse than death, the annihilation of one's identity. . . . What is symbolized as a virgin is actually a human conviction, however expressed, that there is something at the core on one's infinitely fragile being which is not only immortal but has discovered the secret of invulnerability that eludes the tragic hero" (*The Secular Scripture*).

Now let us consolidate what we know in this sketch so far. We have to think in this play not merely about marriage but about the marriage of a romantic hero and of a Christian man, one whose imagination has to incorporate the idea of two becoming one in marriage and the idea that it is better to marry than to burn. It is a play, though it is thought of as domestic, in which not a marriage but an idea of marriage, or let us say an imagination of marriage, is worked out. "Why did I marry?" is the first question Othello asks himself, to express his first raid of suspicion (3.3.242). The question has never been from his mind. Iago's first question to him is "Are you fast married?" and Othello's first set speech ends with something less than an answer: "But that I love the gentle Desdemona, / I would not my unhoused free condition / Put into circumscription and confine / For the sea's worth." Love is at most a necessary, not a sufficient, condition for marrying. And for some minds, a certain idea of love may compromise as much as validate the idea of marriage. It may be better, but it is not perfect to marry, as Saint Paul implies.

We have, further, to think in this play not merely generally of marriage but specifically of the wedding night. It is with this that the play opens. The central fact we know is that the whole beginning scene takes place while Othello and Desdemona are in their bridal bed. The simultaneity is marked: "Even now, now, very now, an old black ram / Is tupping your white ewe" (1.1.88). And the scene is one of treachery, alarms, of shouts, of armed men running through a sleeping city. The conjunction of the bridal chamber with a scene of emergency is again insisted on by Othello's reappearance from his bedroom to stop a brawl with his single presence; a reappearance repeated the first night in Cyprus. As though an appearance from his place of sex and dreams is what gives him the power to stop an armed fight with a word and a gesture. Or is this more than we know? Perhaps the conjunction is to imply that their "hour of love" (1.3.299–300), or their two hours, have each time been interrupted. There is reason to believe that the marriage has not been consummated, anyway reason to believe that Othello does not know whether it has. What is Iago's "Are you fast married?" asking? Whether a public, legal ceremony has taken place or whether a private act; or whether the public and the private have ratified one another? Othello answers by speaking of his nobility and his love. But apart from anything else this seems to assume that Iago's "you" was singular, not plural. And what does Othello mean in Cyprus by these apparently public words:

> Come, my dear love,
> The purchase made, the fruits are to ensue—
> The profit's yet to come 'tween me and you.
> (2.3.8–10)

What is the purchase and what the fruits or profit? Othello has just had proclaimed a general celebration at once of the perdition of the Turkish fleet and of his nuptials (2.2). If the fruits and profit is the resumption of their privacy, then the purchase was the successful discharge of his public office and his entry into Cyprus. But this success was not his doing; it was provided by a tempest. Is the purchase their (public) marriage? Then the fruits and profit is their conjugal love. Then he is saying that this is yet to come. It seems to me possible that the purchase, or price, was her virginity, and the fruits or profit their pleasure. There could hardly be greater emphasis on their having had just one shortened night together, isolated from this second night by a tempest (always in these matters symbolic, perhaps here of a memory, perhaps of an anticipation). Or is it, quite simply, that this is something he wishes to *say* publicly, whatever the truth between them? (How we imagine Desdemona's reaction to this would then become all important.)

I do not think that we must, or that we can, choose among these possibilities in Othello's mind. Rather, I think Othello cannot choose among them. My guiding hypothesis about the structure of the play is that the thing *denied our sight* throughout the opening scene—the thing, the scene, that Iago takes Othello back to again and again, retouching it for Othello's enchafed imagination—is what we are shown in the final scene, the scene of murder. This becomes our ocular proof of Othello's understanding of his two nights of married love. (It has been felt from Thomas Rymer to G. B. Shaw that the play obeys the rhythm of farce, not of tragedy. One might say that in beginning with a sexual scene denied our sight, this play opens exactly as a normal comedy closes, as if it turned comedy inside out.) I will follow out this hypothesis here only to the extent of commenting on that final scene.

However one seeks to interpret the meaning of the great entering speech of the scene ("It is the cause, it is the cause, my soul. . . . Put out the light, and then put out the light" [5.2.1,7]), I cannot take its mysteries, its privacies, its magniloquence, as separate from some massive denial to which these must be in service. Othello must mean that he is acting impersonally, but the words are those of a man in a trance, in a dream-state, fighting not to awaken; willing for anything but light. By "denial" here I do not initially mean something requiring psychoanalytical, or any other, theory. I mean merely to ask that we not, conventionally but insufferably, assume that we know this woman better than this man knows her—making Othello some kind of exotic, gorgeous, superstitious lunkhead; which is about what Iago thinks. However much Othello deserves each of these titles, however far he believes Iago's tidings, he cannot just believe them; somewhere he also *knows* them to be false. This is registered in the rapidity with which he is brought to the truth, with no further real evidence, with only a counterstory (about the handkerchief) that bursts over him, or from him, as the truth. Shall we say he recognizes the truth too late? The fact is, he recognizes it when he is ready to, as one alone can; in this case, when its burden is dead. I am not claiming that he is trying not to believe Iago, or wants not to believe what Iago has told him. (This might describe someone who, say, had a good opinion of Desdemona, not someone whose life is staked upon hers.) I am claiming, on the contrary, that we must understand Othello to be wanting to believe Iago, to be trying, against his knowledge, to believe him. Othello's eager insistence on Iago's honesty, his eager slaking of his thirst for knowledge with that poison, is not a sign of his stupidity in the presence of poison but of his devouring need of it. I do not quite say that he could not have accepted slander about Desdemona so quickly, to the quick, unless he already believed it; but rather that it is a thing he would rather believe than something yet more terrible to his mind; that the idea of Desdemona as an adulterous whore is more convenient to him than the idea of her as chaste. But what could be more terrible than Desdemona's faithlessness? Evidently her faithfulness. But how?

Note that in taking Othello's entering speech as part of a ritual of denial, in the context of taking the murder scene as a whole to be a dream-enactment of the invisible opening of the play, we have an answer implied to our original question about this play, concerning Othello's turning of Desdemona to stone. His image denies that he scarred her and shed her blood. It is a denial at once that he has taken her virginity and that she has died of him. The whole scene of murder is built on the concept of sexual intercourse or orgasm as a dying. There is a dangerously explicit quibble to this effect in the exchange,

> OTHELLO: Thou art on thy death bed.
> DESDEMONA: Aye, but not yet to die.
> (5.2.51–52)

The possible quibble only heightens the already heartbreaking poignance of the wish to die in her marriage bed after a long life.

Though Desdemona no more understands Othello's accusation of her than, in his darkness to himself, he does, she obediently shares his sense that this is their final night and that it is to be some dreamlike recapitulation of their former two nights. This shows in her premonitions of death (the Willow Song, and the request that one of the wedding sheets be her shroud) and in her mysterious request to Emilia, "tonight / Lay on my bed my wedding sheets" (4.2.106–7), as if knowing, and faithful to, Othello's private dream of her, herself preparing the scene of her death as Othello, utilizing Iago's stage directions, imagines it must happen ("Do it not with poison, strangle her in her bed, even the bed she hath contaminated." "Good, good. The justice of it pleases. Very good" [4.1.219–23]); as if knowing that only with these sheets on their bed can his dream of her be contested. The dream is of contamination. The fact the dream works upon is the act of deflowering. Othello is reasonably literal about this, as reasonable as a man in a trance can be:

> When I have plucked the rose,
> I cannot give it vital growth again,
> It must needs wither. I'll smell it on the tree.
> Ah, balmy breath, that dost almost persuade
> Justice to break her sword! One more, one more.
> Be thus when thou art dead, and I will kill thee,
> And love thee after.
>
> (5.2.13–19)

(Necrophilia is an apt fate for a mind whose reason is suffocating in its sumptuous capacity for figuration, and which takes the dying into love literally to entail killing. "That death's unnatural that kills for loving" [5.2.42]; or that turns its object to live stone. It is apt as well that Desdemona sense death, or the figure of death, as the impending cause of death. And at the very end, facing himself, he will not recover from this. "I kissed thee ere I killed thee." And after too. And not just now when you died from me, but on our previous nights as well.)

The exhibition of wedding sheets in this romantic, superstitious, conventional environment, can only refer to the practice of proving purity by staining. I mention in passing that this provides a satisfactory weight for the importance Othello attaches to his charmed (or farcical) handkerchief, the fact that it is spotted, spotted with strawberries.

Well, were the sheets stained or not? Was she a virgin or not? The answers seem as ambiguous as to our earlier question whether they are fast married. Is the final, fatal reenactment of their wedding night a clear denial of what really happened, so that we can just read off, by negation, what really happened? Or is it a straight reenactment, without negation, and the flower was still on the tree, as far as he knew? In that case, who was reluctant to see it plucked, he or she? On such issues, farce and tragedy are separated by the thickness of a membrane.

We of course have no answer to such questions. But what matters is that Othello has no answer; or rather he can give none, for any answer to the question, granted that I am right in taking the question to be his, is intolerable. The torture of logic in his mind we might represent as follows: Either I shed her blood and scarred her or I did not. If I did not then she was not a virgin and this is a stain upon me. If I did then she is no longer a virgin and this is a stain upon me. Either way I am contaminated. (I do not say that the sides of this dilemma are of equal significance for Othello.)

But this much logic anyone but a lunkhead might have mastered apart from actually marrying. (He himself may say as much when he asks himself, too late, why he married.) Then what quickens this logic for him? Call whatever it is Iago. What is Iago?

He is everything, we know, Othello is not. Critical and witty, for example, where Othello is commanding and eloquent; retentive where the other is lavish; concealed where the other is open; cynical where the other is romantic; conventional where the other is original; imagines flesh where the other imagines spirit; the imaginer and manager of the human guise; the bottom end of the world. And so on. A Christian has to call him devil. The single fact between Othello and Iago I focus on here is that Othello fails twice at the end to kill Iago, knowing he cannot kill him. This all but all-powerful chieftain is stopped at this nobody. It is the point of his impotence, and the meaning of it. Iago is everything Othello must deny, and which, denied, is not killed but works on, like poison, like furies.

In speaking of the point and meaning of Othello's impotence, I do not think of Othello as having been in an everyday sense impotent with Desdemona. I think of him, rather, as having been surprised by her, at what he has elicited from her; at, so to speak, a success rather than a failure. It is the dimension of her that shows itself in that difficult and dirty banter between her and Iago as they await Othello on Cyprus. Rather than imagine himself to have elicited that, or solicited it, Othello would imagine it elicited by anyone and everyone else. Surprised, let me say, to find that she is flesh and blood. It was the one thing he could not imagine for himself. For if she is flesh and blood then, since they are one, so is he. But then although his potency of imagination can command the imagination of this child who is everything he is not, so that she sees his visage in his mind, she also sees that he is not identical with his mind, he is more than his imagination, black with desire, which she desires. Iago knows it, and Othello cannot bear what Iago knows, so he cannot outface the way in which he knows it, or knows anything. He cannot forgive her for existing, for being separate from him, outside, beyond command, commanding, her captain's captain.

It is an unstable frame of mind which compounds figurative with literal dying in love; and Othello unstably projects upon her, as he blames her:

> O perjured woman! Thou dost stone thy heart,
> And makest me call what I intend to do
> A murder, which I thought a sacrifice.
>
> (5.2.63–65)

As he is the one who gives out lies about her, so he is the one who will give her a stone heart for her stone body, as if in his words of stone which confound the figurative and the literal there is the confounding of the incantations of poetry and of magic. He makes of her the thing he feels ("my heart is turned to stone" [4.1.193]), but covers the ugliness of his thought with the beauty of his imagery—a debasement of himself and of his art of words. But what produces the idea of sacrifice? How did he manage the thought of her death as a sacrifice? To what was he to sacrifice her? To his image of himself and of her, to keep his image intact, uncontaminated; as if *this* were his protection from slander's image of him, say from a conventional view of his blackness. So he becomes conventional, sacrificing love to convention. But this was unstable; it could not be said. Yet better thought than the truth, which was that the central sacrifice of romance has already been made by them: her virginity, her intactness, her perfection, had been gladly foregone by her for him, for the sake of their union, for the seaming of it. It is the sacrifice he could not accept, for then he was not himself perfect. It must be displaced. The scar is the mark of finitude, of separateness; it must be borne whatever one's anatomical condition, or color. It is the sin or the sign of refusing imperfection that produces, or justifies, the visions and torments of devils that inhabit the region of this play.

If such a man as Othello is rendered impotent and murderous by aroused, or by having aroused, female sexuality; or let us say: if this man is horrified by human sexuality, in himself and in others; then no human being is free of this possibility. What I have wished to bring out is the nature of this possibility, or the possibility of this nature, the way human sexuality is the field in which the fantasy of finitude, of its acceptance and its repetitious overcoming, is worked out; the way human separateness is turned equally toward splendor and toward horror, mixing beauty and ugliness; turned toward before and after; toward flesh and blood. In "Knowing and Acknowledging" I take the skeptical wish as one of interpreting "a metaphysical finitude as an intellectual lack." Is this a denial of the human or an expression of it? For of course there are those for whom the denial of the human *is* the human. Call this the Christian view. It would be why Nietzsche undertook to identify the task of overcoming the human with the task of overcoming the denial of the human; which implies overcoming the human not through mortification but through joy, say ecstasy. If the former can be thought of as the denial of the body then the latter may be thought of as the affirmation of the body. Then those who are pushed, in attempting to counter a dualistic view of mind and body, to assert the identity of body and mind, are skipping or converting the problem. For suppose my identity with my body is something that exists only in my affirmation of my body. Then the question is: What would the body *become* under affirmation? And what would become of *me*?

I conclude with two thoughts, or perspectives, from which to survey one's space of conviction in the reading I have started of *Othello*, and from which perhaps to guide it further.

First, what you might call the philosophy or the moral of the play seems all but contained in the essay Montaigne entitles "On some verses of Virgil," in such a remark as: "What a monstrous animal to be a horror to himself, to be burdened by his pleasures, to regard himself as a misfortune!" The essay concerns the compatibility of sex with marriage, of sex with age; it remarks upon, and upon the relations among, jealousy, chastity, imagination, doubts about virginity; upon the strength of language and the honesty of language; and includes mention of a Turk and of certain instances of necrophilia. One just about runs through the topics of *Othello* if to this essay one adds the essay "Of the power of imagination," which contains a Moor and speaks of a king of Egypt who, finding himself impotent with his bride, threatened to kill her, thinking it was some sort of sorcery. The moral would be what might have been contained in Othello's "one that lov'd not wisely, but too well," that all these topics should be food for thought and moderation, not for torture and murder; as fit for rue and laughter as for pity and terror; that they are not tragic unless one makes them so, takes them so; that we are tragic in what we take to be tragic; that one must take one's imperfections with a "gay and sociable wisdom" (as in Montaigne's "Of experience") not with a somber and isolating eloquence. It is advice to accept one's humanity, and one can almost see Iago as the slanderer of human nature (this would be his diabolism) braced with Othello as the enacter of the slander—the one thinking to escape human nature from below, the other from above. But to whom is the advice usable? And how do we understand why it cannot be taken by those in directest need of it? The urging of moderation is valuable only to the extent that it results from a knowledge of the human possibilities beyond its urging. Is Montaigne's attitude fully earned, itself without a tint of the wish for exemption from the human? Or is Shakespeare's topic of the sheets and the handkerchief understandable as a rebuke to Montaigne, for refusing a further nook of honesty? A bizarre question, I suppose; but meant only to indicate how one might, and why one should, test whether my emphasis on the stain is necessary to give sufficient weight to one's experience of the horror and the darkness of these words and actions, or whether it is imposed.

My second concluding thought is more purely speculative, and arises in response to my having spoken just now of "the refusal of imperfection" as producing "the visions and torments of devils that inhabit the region of this play." I do not wish to dispute the evidence marshalled by Bernard Spivack in his *Shakespeare and the Allegory of Evil* showing Iago to be a descendent of the late morality figure of the Vice. I mean rather to help explain further the appearance of that figure in this particular play, and, I guess, to suggest its humanizing, or human splitting off (the sort of interpretation Spivack's book seems to deplore). It is against the tradition of the morality play that I now go on to call attention—I cannot think I am the first to say it out loud—to the hell and the demon staring out of the names of Othello and Desdemona. I mention this curiosity to prepare something meant as a nearly pure conjecture, wishing others to prove it one way or another, namely that underlying and shaping the events of this play are certain events of witch trials. Phrases such as "the ocular proof" and "cords, or knives / Poison, or fire, or suffocating streams" (3.3.388–89) seem to me to call for location in a setting of legal torture. And I confess to finding myself thinking of Desdemona's haunting characterization of a certain conception of her as "a moth of peace" when I read, from an 1834 study called *Folk-lore of the NE of Scotland*, "In some parts of Scotland moths are called 'witches' " (quoted in Kittredge, *Witchcraft in Old and New England*). But what prompts my thought primarily is the crazed logic Othello's rage for proof and for "satisfaction" seems to require (like testing for a woman's witchcraft by seeing whether she will drown, declaring that if she does she was innocent but if she does not she is to be put to death for a witch): What happened on our wedding night is that I killed her; but she is not dead; therefore she is not human; therefore she must die. ("Yet she must die, else she'll betray more men" [5.2.6].) Again he claims not to be acting personally, but by authority; here he has delivered a sentence. I recall that the biblical justification for the trial of witches was familiarly from the punishments in Exodus: "Thou shalt not suffer a witch to live." Othello seems to be babbling the crazed logic as he falls into his explicit faint or trance: "First to be hanged, and then to confess. I tremble at it" (4.1.38–39), not knowing whether he is torturer or victim.

I introduced the idea of the trial for witchcraft as a conjecture, meaning immediately that it is not meant as a hypothesis: I do not *require* it for any interpretative alignment of my senses with the world of this play. It is enough, without supposing Shakespeare to have cribbed from literal subtexts of this sort, that the play opens with a public accusation of witchcraft, and an abbreviated trial, and is then succeeded with punctuating thoughts of hell and by fatal scenes of psychological torture, and concludes with death as the proof of mortality, that is, of innocence (compare, "If that thou be'st a devil, I cannot kill thee" [5.2.287]). Enough, I mean, to stir the same depths of superstition—of a horror that proposes our lack of certain access to other minds—that under opportune institutions caused trials of witchcraft. The play is at once, as we would expect of what we call Shakespeare's humanity, an examination of the madness and bewitchment of inquisitors, as well as of the tortures of love; of those tortures of which both victim and torturer are victims.

A statue, a stone, is something whose existence is fundamentally open to the ocular proof. A human being is not. The two bodies lying together on their bridal and death sheets form an emblem of this fact, the truth of skepticism. What this man lacked was not certainty. He knew everything, but he could not yield to what he knew, be commanded by it. He found out too much for his mind, not too little. Their differences from one another—the one everything the other is not—form an emblem of human separation, which can be accepted, and granted, or not. Like the dissociation from God; everything we are not.

# Beyond Comedy: *Othello*

*Susan Snyder*

To the extent that Shakespeare allowed bad luck to defeat love in *Romeo and Juliet*, we may see him as questioning comic assumptions in that play, but the questioning does not go very deep. The lovers' relationship is presented as natural and right in itself. If it makes them irrationally impetuous, it is nevertheless not this rashness that precipitates the tragedy. In *Othello*, however, Shakespeare subjects the comic assumptions about the love union, nature, and reason to a radical reassessment, and in so doing exposes the roots of tragedy.

Just as such a scrutiny logically comes *after* the first unquestioning acceptance, so Othello's and Desdemona's story is deliberately set up as postcomic. Courtship and ratified marriage, the whole story of comedy, appear in *Othello* as a preliminary to tragedy. The play's action up until the reunion of Othello and Desdemona in Cyprus (2.1) is a perfect comic structure in miniature. The wooing that the two of them describe in the Venetian council scene (1.3) has succeeded in spite of barriers of age, color, and condition of life; the machinations of villain and doltish rival have come to nothing; the blocking father has been overruled by the good duke; and nature has cooperated in the general movement with a storm that disperses the last external threat, the Turks, while preserving the favored lovers. Othello's reunion speech to Desdemona underlines this sense of a movement accomplished, a still point of happiness like the final scene of a comedy:

---

From *The Comic Matrix of Shakespeare's Tragedies*. © 1979 by Princeton University Press.

> If it were now to die,
> 'Twere now to be most happy; for I fear
> My soul hath her content so absolute
> That not another comfort like to this
> Succeeds in unknown fate.
>
> (2.1.187–91)

But at the same time that Othello celebrates his peak of joy so markedly, his invocations of death, fear, and unknown fate make us apprehensive about the postcomic future. Desdemona's equally negative mode of agreement ("The heavens forbid / But that our loves and comforts should increase") indirectly reinforces this unease, and Iago's threat does so directly: "O, you are well tun'd now! / But I'll set down the pegs that make this music." In these few lines Shakespeare prepares us for tragedy, in part by announcing the end of comedy. The happy ending is completed, and Othello and Desdemona are left to go on from there.

If I am right to see the tragedy of *Othello* developing from a questioning of comic assumptions, then the initial comic movement ought to make us aware of unresolved tensions in this successful love. And it does, in various ways. Othello's account of their shy, story-telling courtship, however moving and beautiful, is in retrospect disturbing. "She lov'd me for the dangers I had pass'd; / And I lov'd her that she did pity them" (1.3.167–68) [All *Othello* citations are to *The Complete Works of Shakespeare*, ed. Peter Alexander]. Is it enough? Some critics have on this hint proclaimed the Moor totally self-centered, incapable of real love. This is surely too severe. Nevertheless, in his summary their love has a proxy quality. "The dangers I had pass'd" have served as a counter between them, a substitute for direct engagement or, at best, a preliminary to something not yet achieved. Twice before, Shakespeare had used comedy to explore the inadequacies of romantic courtship, cursorily in *Taming of the Shrew* and more thoroughly in *Much Ado About Nothing*. In the latter play, Claudio and Hero move through the paces of conventional wooing, depending on rumors and go-betweens, without direct exploration of each other's nature. Thus, Hero can be traduced and Claudio can believe it, lacking as he does the knowledge of the heart that should counteract the false certainty of the eyes. *Much Ado* is a comedy, and thus the presiding deities give time for Dogberry's muddled detective work and provide in the Friar a benevolent countermanipulator against Don John. The love of Othello and Desdemona has the same vulnerability, but no time is given; and instead of Friar Francis, Iago is in charge.

Iago is the most obvious potential force for tragedy in the early part of the play. We see him thwarted in his first plot against Othello but already, at the end of act 1, planning the next. His speech at this point suggests in both overt statement and imagery the thrust beyond the comic, the germination out of the first failure of a deeper evil:

> I ha't—it is engender'd. Hell and night
> Must bring this monstrous birth to the world's light.
> (1.3.397–98)

It was Bradley, expanding on suggestions from Hazlitt and Swinburne, who compared Iago in his first two soliloquies to a playwright in the early stages of writing a new play—"drawing at first only an outline, puzzled how to fix more than the main idea, and gradually seeing it develop and clarify as he works upon it or lets it work." Bradley's parallel highlights the unexpected kinship between Iago and the magicians and friars of comedy, who arrange "fond pageants" in which other characters play unaware the parts assigned to them, and who dispose events toward the desired ending as a dramatist does. The implication that a single human being can control persons and change realities, exhilarating within the safe parameters of comedy, is sinister here.

So is the holiday from reason that comedy proclaims for romantic love. Iago is the most intelligent character in the play, and reason—or the appearance of reason—is his chief means of controlling others. The *power* of the rational view, in the comedies so easily dismissed with laughter or overruled by emotion, is grimly realized in Iago's accurate estimates of character

> The Moor is of a free and open nature
> That thinks men honest that but seem to be so;
> And will as tenderly be led by th' nose . . .
> (1.3.393–95)

his telling arguments from experience

> In Venice they do let God see the pranks
> They dare not show their husbands
> . . . . . . . . . . . . . .
> She did deceive her father, marrying you
> (3.3.206–10)

his plausible hypotheses

> That Cassio loves her, I do well believe it;
> That she loves him, 'tis apt and of great credit
> (2.1.280–81)

and his final triumph in converting Othello to the philosophy of "ocular proof" (3.3.364). Against him the love of Othello and Desdemona is vulnerable, rooted as it is not in rational evaluation of empirical knowledge but in instinctive sympathy. The same scene that underlines how indirect was their courtship (1.3) also brings out the peculiar strength of their love that is a weakness as well:

> DESDEMONA: I saw Othello's visage in his mind.
> (1.252)
>
> OTHELLO: My life upon her faith!
> (1.294)

There is a core of power in this instinctive mutual recognition that survives Iago's rational poison and in a sense defeats it, but this victory comes only in death. In his posing of Iago against Othello and Desdemona, Shakespeare fully explores the conventional dichotomy between reason and love and uncovers its deeply tragic implications.

If reason's opposition to love is traditional, nature in *Othello* appears to have changed sides. Love's ally is now love's enemy, partly because the angle of vision has changed: nature as instinctual rightness gives way to nature as abstract concept, susceptible like all concepts to distortion and misapplication. Brabantio, Iago, and finally Othello himself see the love between Othello and Desdemona as *un*natural—"nature erring from itself" (3.3.231). But there is more to it than this. In key scenes of *Othello* a tension develops between two senses of *nature*, the general and the particular.

It is to general nature, the common experience and prejudice by which like calls only to like, that Brabantio appeals in the Venetian council scene. An attraction between the young white Venetian girl and the aging black foreigner, since it goes against this observed law of nature, could only have been "wrought" by unnatural means.

> She is abus'd, stol'n, from me, and corrupted,
> By spells and medicines bought of mountebanks;
> For nature so preposterously to err,
> Being not deficient, blind, or lame of sense,
> Sans witchcraft could not.
> (1.3.60–64)

The other sense of *nature* is particular and personal. What Iago means in his soliloquy at the end of this scene when he says the Moor "is of a free and open nature" is individual essence: the inscape of Othello. Brabantio tries to bring in this nature to support the other in his appeal against the marriage. He says that Desdemona is essentially timid, thus by nature (her own) cannot love the fearsome Moor.

> A maiden never bold,
> Of spirit so still and quiet that her motion
> Blush'd at herself; and she—in spite of nature,
> Of years, of country, credit, every thing—
> To fall in love with what she fear'd to look on!
> It is a judgment maim'd and most imperfect
> That will confess perfection so could err
> Against all rules of nature.
> (1.3.94–101)

But this personal nature is the very ground of Desdemona's love. In her answer to her father and the Venetian Senate she tells how, penetrating through the blackness and strangeness, she saw Othello's true visage in his mind and subdued her heart to that essence, his "very quality."

For Desdemona, then, nature as individual essence is not the enemy of love. But Iago has the last word in this scene, and his conclusion is ominous: Othello's very generosity and openness will make him take the appearance of honesty for the fact. That is, Othello will act instinctively according to the laws of his own nature rather than according to reasoned evaluation (which would perceive that most liars pretend to be telling the truth). This internal law of nature, then, implies the same vulnerability that we have seen in the instinctive, nonrational quality of Othello's and Desdemona's love.

Brabantio's general nature is implicitly reductive in that it derives rules for individuals from the behavior of the herd. Iago's is explicitly reductive. For him "the herd" is no metaphor, and the view he expounds to Roderigo has no place for human values or ethical norms. Natural law for Iago, as for Edmund in *King Lear*, is Hobbesian—a matter of animal appetites promoted by cleverness, with the strongest and the shrewdest winning out. Desdemona, he assures Roderigo, will tire of Othello because the appetite requires fresh stimuli:

> Her eye must be fed; and what delight shall she have to look on the devil? When the blood is made dull with the act of sport, there should be—again to inflame it, and to give satiety a fresh appetite—loveliness in favour, sympathy in years, manners, and beauties—all which the Moor is defective in. Now for want of these requir'd conveniences, her delicate tenderness will find itself abus'd, begin to heave the gorge, disrelish and abhor the

> Moor; very nature will instruct her in it, and compel her to some second choice.
>
> (2.1.221–33)

*Compel* her—here is yet another "law," generalized from the ways of animal nature. The context is wholly physical, as the persistent images of eating and disgorging keep reminding us. Iago has begun the discussion by prodding on the hesitant lover Roderigo with a bit of folk wisdom: "They say base men being in love have then a nobility in their natures more than is native to them" (ll. 212–14). But he does not pretend to believe it himself. Love is rather "a lust of the blood and a permission of the will"; Roderigo, in love or not, is a snipe; our natures are "blood and baseness." In Iago's determined animalism there is another unexpected reminder of comedy, this time of the antiromantic servant or rustic whose imagination is bounded by the physical. It is perhaps because this view can be destructive when actually *acted out* against idealized love that the clowns of comedy are kept largely apart from the plot, as onlookers. Iago is a clown without good humor and (what underlies that lack) without self-sufficiency, who must therefore prove his theories on other people. Interestingly, this transfer of the debunking low-life perspective to the service of active malevolence seems to have left no function for the play's official clown. His feeble essays at bawdry and wordplay have nothing conceptual to adhere to, and after a second brief appearance in act 2 he departs unmourned.

In Shakespeare's portrayal of Iago we can see a version of the clash I have been describing. In spite of his reductive general view, he can recognize the essential goodness of Othello ("free and open nature," "constant, loving, noble nature") as well as Desdemona's generosity and the daily beauty of Cassio's life. Critics have complained of the inconsistency, and if *Othello* were naturalistic drama, they would be right to do so. But Iago is not just an envious spoiler; he is the symbolic enemy of love itself. The play's conception demands that the weapons of both "natures," like those of reason, be put in his hands.

In his great self-summation at the play's end, Othello says he was "wrought" from his true nature, and so he was. His own nature, noble and trusting, gave him an instinctive perception of Desdemona's, a perception which breaks forth at the sight of her even while Iago is poisoning his mind: "If she be false, O, then heaven mocks itself! / I'll not believe it" (3.3.282–83). But Iago is able to undermine that trust with false rationality, the insistence that Desdemona's honor, which is "an essence that's not seen," be made susceptible of ocular proof. He succeeds, where Brabantio failed, in using both conceptions of nature against Othello. The Moor's own generous nature, Iago suggests, makes him an easy dupe. "I would not have your free and noble nature / Out of self-bounty be abus'd; look to 't" (ll. 203–4). Taught to look from the outside instead of trust from the inside, Othello soon sees Desdemona's choice of him as an aberration, nature erring from itself. Iago quickly advances the other nature, the law of all things, to reinforce the idea:

> Ay, there's the point: as—to be bold with you—
> Not to affect many proposed matches
> Of her own clime, complexion, and degree,
> Whereto we see in all things nature tends—
> Foh! one may smell in such a will most rank,
> Foul disproportion, thoughts unnatural.
> (ll. 232–37)

And so Othello violates his own peculiar essence and internalizes Iago's law of the many. Desdemona soon realizes uneasily that he is altered ("My lord is not my lord": 3.4.125) and, in an ironic reflection of Othello's confusion, seeks the explanation in a generalization about "men": "Men's natures wrangle with inferior things, / Though great ones are their object" (ll. 145–46). Later the Venetian visitors gaze horrified at the change in that nature that passion could not shake, as Othello strikes his wife and then exits mumbling of goats and monkeys. He has taken into himself Iago's reductive view of man as animal. In the next scene (4.2) he will see Desdemona in terms of toads coupling and maggots quickening in rotten meat.

The love that in comedies was a strength in *Othello* is vulnerable to attacks of reason, arguments from nature. More than that: vulnerability is its very essence. Before falling in love with Desdemona, Othello was self-sufficient, master of himself and of the battlefield. After he believes her to be false, his occupation is gone. Why? Because love has created a dependency, a yielding of the separate, sufficient self to incorporation with another. What comedy treated as a liberating completeness becomes in *Othello* the heart of tragedy. Even in the play's comic phase there are signs of this new and potentially dangerous vulnerability. Othello's images for his love-commitment are not of expansion but of narrowing and confining:

> But that I love the gentle Desdemona,
> I would not my unhoused free condition
> Put into circumscription and confine
> For the seas' worth.
> (1.2.25–28)

To love totally is to give up the freedom of self for the perils of union, and the expansive great world for an other-centered, contingent one. Othello makes a significant metaphor for Desdemona near the end of the play:

> Nay, had she been true,
> If heaven would make me *such another world*
> Of one entire and perfect chrysolite,
> I'd not have sold her for it.

"My life upon her faith" is literally true. Desdemona has become Othello's world.

It is in this light, I think, that we can best understand why Othello reacts to Iago's insinuations about Desdemona by renouncing his profession. The great aria on military life invokes, not chaos and carnage, but *order*. War is individual passion subordinated to a larger plan, martial harmony, formal pageantry, imitation of divine judgment.

> O, now for ever
> Farewell the tranquil mind! farewell content!
> Farewell the plumed troops, and the big wars
> That makes ambition virtue! O, farewell!
> Farewell the neighing steed and the shrill trump,
> The spirit-stirring drum, th' ear-piercing fife,
> The royal banner, and all quality,
> Pride, pomp, and circumstance, of glorious war!
> And O ye mortal engines whose rude throats
> Th' immortal Jove's dread clamours counterfeit,
> Farewell! Othello's occupation's gone.
> (3.3.35–61)

Stylistically and rhythmically, the formal catalogues and ritual repetitions strengthen this selective picture of war as majestic order. Earlier in this scene Othello has said that when he stops loving Desdemona, chaos will come again. Now it has happened. With his world thrown into chaos, his ordering generalship is gone.

Othello's disintegration of self is the dark side of comedy's rejection of singleness, its insistence on completing oneself with another. But Shakespeare goes deeper in his exploration of comic assumptions by showing that the desired merging of self and other is in any case impossible. The more or less schematized pairings-off of the comedies combine necessary opposition (male / female) with sympathies in age, background, temperament. It is enough in comedy to suggest compatibility by outward signs and look no farther than the formal union. But in *Othello* Shakespeare has taken pains in several ways to emphasize the separateness of his lovers.

Cinthio's Moor in the source tale is handsome, apparently fairly young, and a longtime Venetian resident. Apart from sex, his only real difference from Desdemona is one of color, and Cinthio does not dwell on it much. Shakespeare dwells on it a great deal. Black-white oppositions weave themselves continually into the verbal fabric of *Othello*. Indeed, the blackness of Cinthio's hero may have been one of the story's main attractions for Shakespeare. Certainly he altered other details of the story to reinforce this paradigmatic separation into black and white, to increase Othello's alienness and widen the gulf between his experience and Desdemona's. Shakespeare's Moor is a stranger to Venice and to civil life in general; his entire career, except for the brief period in which he courted Desdemona, has been spent in camp and on the battlefield (1.3.83–87). Even Othello's speech reminds us constantly, if subtly, of his apartness. It is hardly rude, as he claims to the Venetian Senate, but it is certainly different from theirs. His idiom naturally invokes Anthropophagi and Pontic seas, roots itself in the exotic rather than the everyday social life that is familiar to the others but not to him. He knows as little of Venetian ways as Desdemona knows of "antres vast and deserts idle," and he is given no time to learn. While Cinthio's Moor and his bride live for some time in Venice after their marriage, Othello and Desdemona must go at once to Cyprus—and not even in the same ship. No wonder that, when Iago generalizes about the habits of his countrywomen ("In Venice they do let God see the pranks / They dare not show their husbands"), Othello can only respond helplessly, "Dost thou say so?" (3.3.206–9). Shakespeare has deprived him of any common ground with Desdemona on which he can stand to fight back—not only to facilitate Iago's deception, but to heighten the tragic paradox of human love, individuals dependent on each other but unalterably separate and mysterious to one another in their separateness. The two great values of comic convention—love and the fuller self—are seen as tragically incompatible.

To sharpen the contrast, Othello is made middle-aged, thick-lipped—everything Desdemona is not. The image of black man and white girl in conjunction, so repellent to some critics that they had to invent a tawny or café-au-lait Moor, is at the center of the play's conception of disjunction in love. It gives visual focus to the other oppositions of war and peace, age and youth, man and woman. This disjunction serves the plot: it assists

Iago's initial deception, and it provides most of the tension in the period between the deception and the murder, as Desdemona inopportunely pleads for Cassio, and Othello in turn can communicate his fears only indirectly, through insults and degradations. But beyond this plot function the disjunction constitutes a tragic vision of love itself.

What I am suggesting is that the action of *Othello* moves us not only as a chain of events involving particular people as initiators and victims, but also as an acting out of the tragic implications in any love relationship. Iago is an envious, insecure human being who functions as a perverted magician-manipulator, cunningly altering reality for Othello. But he is also the catalyst who activates destructive forces not of his own creation, forces present in the love itself. His announcement of the "monstrous birth" quoted above has special significance in this regard. Coming at the end of a resolved marriage scene, it implies that the monster will be the product of the marriage. Iago says, "It is engender'd," not "I have engendered it," because he is not parent but midwife. "Hell and night," embodied in this demi-devil who works in the dark, will bring the monster forth, but it is the fruit of love itself.

Because *Othello* is a play, and a great one, tragic action and tragic situation are fully fused in it, and it would be pointless to try to separate them. But a look at some of Shakespeare's nondramatic work may help clarify the paradoxical sense of love as both life and destruction that informs the events of this play. The sonnets present a range of attitudes to love, from joyous assurance to disgust and despair, but they return again and again to a certain kind of tension between lover and beloved. Sonnet 57 is one example.

> Being your slave, what should I do but tend
> Upon the hours and times of your desire?
> I have no precious time at all to spend,
> Nor services to do, till you require.
> Nor dare I chide the world-without-end hour,
> Whilst I, my sovereign, watch the clock for you,
> Nor think the bitterness of absence sour,
> When you have bid your servant once adieu;
> Nor dare I question with my jealous thought
> Where you may be, or your affairs suppose,
> But, like a sad slave, stay and think of nought
> Save where you are how happy you make those.
> So true a fool is love that in your will,
> Though you do anything, he thinks no ill.

This apparently positive statement belies its own assent to the terms of relationship by double-edged phrases like "no *precious* time" and "Nor *dare* I chide," and by the bitter wordplay of the couplet: "So true a fool" suggests the loyally loving innocent, but also "so absolutely a dupe." "Fool" completes the sonnet's identification of beloved as monarch and lover as slave. He is not just any kind of slave but the king's fool, a hanger-on who is valued for the occasional diversion he provides. The total effect is of a speaker pulled in contrary directions by need of his friend and esteem of himself.

In Sonnet 35, images and syntax convey the cost of commitment in love.

> No more be griev'd at that which thou hast done:
> Roses have thorns, and silver fountains mud;
> Clouds and eclipses stain both moon and sun,
> And loathsome canker lives in sweetest bud.
> All men make faults, and even I in this,
> Authorizing thy trespass with compare,
> Myself corrupting, salving thy amiss,
> Excusing thy sins more than thy sins are;
> For to thy sensual fault I bring in sense—
> Thy adverse party is thy advocate—
> And 'gainst myself a lawful plea commence;
> Such civil war is in my love and hate
> That I an accessary needs must be
> To that sweet thief which sourly robs from me.

The poem strives to repair the damaged relationship by creating a new equality between lover and beloved. It does indeed achieve this, but only at the cost of the speaker's own integrity. He manages to absolve his friend of fault by natural comparisons, nature having no moral dimension to justify blame, and then implicates himself in fault for making those very comparisons—authorizing the trespass with compare. The last part of the sonnet strains against the first quatrain, and in that strain lies its impact. Can we accept the absolution given in lines 1–4 if the mode of absolution turns out to be sinful? The images reinforce this sense of disjunction: those of the first quatrain are drawn exclusively from the natural world, and those of the remainder come from the civilized world of moral man, especially the law courts. "Civil war," finally overt in line 12, is implicit earlier in the like-sounding antitheses that shape lines 7–10 into a series of tensions. The couplet, its message of inner division supported by the difficult twisting of the last line, completes the violation of self that love has required.

The same kind of violation, expressed with less anguish and more wry acceptance, is the theme of Sonnet 138:

> When my love swears that she is made of truth,
> I do believe her, though I know she lies.

Here is a comic response to the problem of integrity compromised by dependence on another, as *Othello* is a tragic response. In its mutual accommodation reached through lies and pretenses, Sonnet 138 also stresses the other side of the paradox, the necessary separateness of lovers. Even the more idealistic sonnets never proclaim complete union. And the most idealistic of all, Sonnet 116, presents quite an opposite picture, of love persisting on its own in spite of the beloved's infidelity:

> Love is not love
> Which alters when it alteration finds,
> Or bends with the remover to remove.
> . . . . . . . . . . . . .
> Love alters not with his brief hours and weeks,
> But bears it out even to the edge of doom.

This is selfless but ultimately single, more like God's love for man than like any human relationship. Edward Hubler saw in Sonnet 116 Shakespeare's affirmation of mutuality as the essence of love. It seems to me just the contrary, a recognition that if love does depend on being requited it will be neither lasting nor true. It must necessarily bend with the remover, meet defection with defection.

Enduring mutuality does not seem to be a possibility in the sonnets. When Shakespeare does address himself to the merging of separate identities, the result is the rarefied allegory of "The Phoenix and Turtle." Here the impossibility is even clearer. The phoenix and the turtle dove are perfectly united, but they are dead. Most of the poem is a dirge sung at their funeral, and it ends in complete stasis—triplets with a single rhyme sound asserting that these lovers left no progeny, that what they represented is gone forever.

> Leaving no posterity—
> 'Twas not their infirmity,
> It was married chastity.

Truth may seem, but cannot be;
Beauty brag, but 'tis not she:
Truth and beauty buried be.

What do we make of this? It has been argued that "The Phoenix and Turtle" approaches "pure poetry" in being all vehicle with no tenor. Certainly it is hard to relate these dead birds and their metaphysical-paradoxical union to the affairs of mortal men and women. Do phoenix and turtle die because annihilation is implicit in perfect union, or because their obliteration of distance, number, and individuality offends against natural law, or because such perfection is possible only outside of time? In any case, the poem makes it clear that the ideal will never again be realized on earth.

The dead-end quality of "The Phoenix and Turtle" illuminates tragic love in *Othello* in one way, as the sonnets' tensions and compromises do in another. The sonnets, indeed, provide the most succinct statement of the dilemma I have been exploring in *Othello*, in the opening lines of Sonnet 36:

Let me confess that we two must be twain,
Although our undivided loves are one.

In his comedies Shakespeare viewed the coming together of incomplete opposites from a certain intellectual distance. In *Othello* he struck a vein of tragedy by focusing on the contradiction within such a conception: denial of self-sufficiency combined with continued isolation in the self. The comic structure at the beginning of *Othello* does not, as in *Romeo and Juliet*, arouse comic expectations. The seeds of tragedy are already there, and Iago threatens in a way that Tybalt could not. Instead, the rather neat comic pattern, glossing over the vulnerabilities and ambiguities in Othello's and Desdemona's love and disposing too opportunely of the implacable forces represented by Iago, sets up a point of departure for what is to follow: the look beyond and beneath comedy.

In calling *Othello* a tragic statement about love in general I do not mean to deny the power and beauty of the relationship between Othello and Desdemona, which the play celebrates fully. The great worth of love is, after all, what makes its internal flaws so painful. Nor do I wish to turn this very human drama into an allegory. But I do suggest that the universal dimension, the wider reverberations that some critics have felt lacking in *Othello*, emerge very clearly when the play is seen from this perspective. We have perhaps spent too much time asking the traditional questions about this play: Is Othello culpable in succumbing to Iago's suggestions?

What makes Iago do what he does? These are important questions, but it is also important to look beyond the individual events of *Othello*, the defeat of a more or less noble dupe by an obscurely motivated villain, to the tragic inadequacies and contradictions of love itself.

Shakespeare's two Italianate tragedies offer companion pictures of the vulnerability of love, threatened from without in *Romeo and Juliet*, from within in *Othello*. It is this concentration on vulnerable *love* that distinguishes these plays from two others where love comes to grief, *Troilus and Cressida* and *Antony and Cleopatra*. Both of the latter present their romantic principals with considerable comic distancing and deflation; that is, their emphasis is on the vulnerability of the *lovers*. *Troilus* is so dominated by the debunking vein, which affects the warriors as well as the lovers, that no sense of the heroic survives in it. Confusion over its genre began in Shakespeare's own time—the quarto title pages called it a history, the author of the 1609 preface praised it as a comedy, the First Folio editors apparently planned to place it among the tragedies—and continues in our own. *Antony*, however, is tragic in form and effect. If I had included it in this study, its proper place would have been between *Hamlet* and *King Lear*. Antony, like Hamlet, suffers from his own largeness of spirit and consequent inability to narrow down, choose, discard alternatives. Like Lear, he exemplifies a special version of the heroic which must justify itself in the face of direct comic attack, of intimations of absurdity. But even this attack is adumbrated in *Hamlet*, which looks forward as well as back in its rich exploitation of comic means for tragic ends.

# The Improvisation of Power

*Stephen Greenblatt*

In Iago's first soliloquy, Shakespeare goes out of his way to emphasize the improvised nature of the villain's plot:

> Cassio's a proper man, let me see now,
> To get this place, and to make up my will,
> A double knavery . . . how, how? . . . let me see,
> After some time, to abuse Othello's ear,
> That he is too familiar with his wife:
> He has a person and a smooth dispose,
> To be suspected, fram'd to make women false:
> The Moor a free and open nature too,
> That thinks men honest that but seems to be so:
> And will as tenderly be led by the nose . . .
> As asses are.
> I ha't, it is engender'd; Hell and night
> Must bring this monstrous birth to the world's light.
> (1.3.390–402)

We will try shortly to cast some light on why Iago conceives of his activity here as sexual; for the moment, we need only to observe all of the marks of the impromptu and provisional, extending to the ambiguity of the third-person pronoun: "to abuse Othello's ear / That he is too familiar with his wife." This ambiguity is felicitous; indeed, though scarcely visible at this point, it is the dark essence of Iago's whole enterprise which is, as

---

we shall see, to play upon Othello's buried perception of his own sexual relations with Desdemona as adulterous.

What I have called the marks of the impromptu extend to Iago's other speeches and actions through the course of the whole play. In act 2, he declares of his conspiracy, " 'tis here, but yet confus'd; / Knavery's plain face is never seen, till us'd," and this half-willed confusion continues through the agile, hectic maneuvers of the last act until the moment of exposure and silence. To all but Roderigo, of course, Iago presents himself as incapable of improvisation, except in the limited and seemingly benign form of banter and jig. And even here, he is careful, when Desdemona asks him to improvise her praise, to declare himself unfit for the task:

> I am about it, but indeed my invention
> Comes from my pate as birdlime does from frieze,
> It plucks out brain and all: but my Muse labours,
> And thus she is deliver'd.
>
> (2.1.125–28)

Lurking in the homely denial of ability is the image of his invention as birdlime, and hence a covert celebration of his power to ensnare others. Like Jonson's Mosca, Iago is fully aware of himself as an improviser and revels in his ability to manipulate his victims, to lead them by the nose like asses, to possess their labor without their ever being capable of grasping the relation in which they are enmeshed. Such is the relation Iago establishes with virtually every character in the play, from Othello and Desdemona to such minor figures as Montano and Bianca. For the Spanish colonialists, improvisation could only bring the Lucayans into open enslavement; for Iago, it is the key to a mastery whose emblem is the "duteous and knee-crooking knave" who dotes "on his own obsequious bondage" (1.1.45–46) [All *Othello* citations are to the Arden Shakespeare edition, ed. M. R. Ridley], a mastery invisible to the servant, a mastery, that is, whose character is essentially ideological. Iago's attitude toward Othello is nonetheless colonial: though he finds himself in a subordinate position, the ensign regards his black general as "an erring barbarian" whose "free and open nature" is a fertile field for exploitation. However galling it may be to him, Iago's subordination is a kind of protection, for it conceals his power and enables him to play upon the ambivalence of Othello's relation to Christian society: the Moor at once represents the institution and the alien, the conqueror and the infidel. Iago can conceal his malicious intentions toward "the thick-lips" behind the mask of dutiful service and hence prolong his improvisation as the Spaniards could not. To be sure, the play suggests, Iago must ultimately destroy the beings he exploits and hence undermine the profitable economy of his own relations, but that destruction may be long deferred, deferred in fact for precisely the length of the play.

If Iago then holds over others a possession that must constantly efface the signs of its own power, how can it be established, let alone maintained? We will find a clue, I think, in what we have been calling [elsewhere] the process of fictionalization that transforms a fixed symbolic structure into a flexible construct ripe for improvisational entry. This process is at work in Shakespeare's play, where we may more accurately identify it as *submission to narrative self-fashioning*. When in Cyprus Othello and Desdemona have been ecstatically reunited, Iago astonishes Roderigo by informing him that Desdemona is in love with Cassio. He has no evidence, of course—indeed we have earlier seen him "engender" the whole plot entirely out of his fantasy—but he proceeds to lay before his gull all of the circumstances that make this adultery plausible: "mark me, with what violence she first lov'd the Moor, but for bragging, and telling her fantastical lies; and she will love him still for prating?" (2.1.221–23). Desdemona cannot long take pleasure in her outlandish match: "When the blood is made dull with the act of sport, there should be again to inflame it, and give satiety a fresh appetite, loveliness in favor, sympathy in years, manners and beauties" (2.1.225–29). The elegant Cassio is the obvious choice: "Didst thou not see her paddle with the palm of his hand?" Iago asks. To Roderigo's objection that this was "but courtesy," Iago replies, "Lechery, by this hand: an index and prologue to the history of lust and foul thoughts" (2.1.251–55). The metaphor makes explicit what Iago has been doing all along: constructing a narrative into which he inscribes ("by this hand") those around him. He does not need a profound or even reasonably accurate understanding of his victims; he would rather deal in probable impossibilities than improbable possibilities. And it is eminently probable that a young, beautiful Venetian gentlewoman would tire of her old, outlandish husband and turn instead to the handsome, young lieutenant: it is, after all, one of the master plots of comedy.

What Iago as inventor of comic narrative needs is a sharp eye for the surfaces of social existence, a sense, as Bergson says, of the mechanical encrusted upon the living, a reductive grasp of human possibilities. These he has in extraordinarily full measure. "The wine she drinks is made of grapes," he says in response to Roderigo's idealization of Desdemona, and so reduced, she can be assimilated to Iago's grasp of the usual run of humanity. Similarly, in a spirit of ironic connoisseurship, he observes Cassio's courtly gestures, "If such tricks as these strip you out of your lieutenantry, it had been better you had not kiss'd your three fingers so oft, which now again you are most apt to play the sir in: good, well kiss'd, an excellent courtesy" (2.1.171–75). He is watching a comedy of manners. Above all, Iago is sensitive to habitual and self-limiting forms of discourse, to Cassio's reaction when he has had a drink or when someone mentions Bianca, to Othello's rhetorical extremism, to Desdemona's persistence and tone when she pleads for a friend; and, of course, he is demonically sensitive to the way individuals interpret discourse, to the signals they ignore and those to which they respond.

We should add that Iago includes himself in this ceaseless narrative invention; indeed, as we have seen from the start, a successful improvisational career depends upon role-playing, which is in turn allied to the capacity, as Professor Lerner defines empathy, "to see oneself in the other fellow's situation." This capacity requires above all a sense that one is not forever fixed in a single, divinely sanctioned identity, a sense Iago expresses to Roderigo in a parodically sententious theory of self-fashioning: "our bodies are gardens, to the which our wills are gardeners, so that if we will plant nettles, or sow lettuce, set hyssop, and weed up thyme; supply it with one gender of herbs, or distract it with many; either to have it sterile with idleness, or manur'd with industry, why, the power, and corrigible authority of this, lies in our wills" (1.3.320–26). Confident in his shaping power, Iago has the role-player's ability to imagine his nonexistence so that he can exist for a moment in another and as another. In the opening scene he gives voice to this hypothetical self-cancellation in a line of eerie simplicity: "Were I the Moor, I would not be Iago" (1.1.57). The simplicity is far more apparent than real. Is the "I" in both halves of the line the same? Does it designate a hard, impacted self-interest prior to social identity, or are there two distinct, even opposing selves? Were I the Moor, I would not be Iago, because the "I" always loves itself and the creature I know as Iago hates the Moor he serves or, alternatively, because as the Moor I would be other than I am now, free of the tormenting appetite and revulsion that characterize the servant's relation to his master and that constitute my identity as Iago. I would be radically the same / I would be radically different; the rapacious ego underlies all institutional structures / the rapacious ego is constituted by institutional structures.

What is most disturbing in Iago's comically banal and fathomless expression—as for that matter, in Professor Lerner's definition of empathy—is that the imagined self-loss conceals its opposite: a ruthless displacement and absorption of the other. Empathy, as the German *Einfühlung* suggests, may be a feeling of oneself into an object, but that object may have to be drained of its own substance before it will serve as an appropriate vessel. Certainly in *Othello*, where all relations are embedded in power and sexuality, there is no realm where the subject and object can merge in the unproblematic accord affirmed by the theorists of empathy. As Iago himself proclaims, his momentary identification with the Moor is a strategic aspect of his malevolent hypocrisy:

> In following him, I follow but myself.
> Heaven is my judge, not I for love and duty,
> But seeming so, for my peculiar end.
> (1.1.58–60)

Exactly what that "peculiar end" is remains opaque. Even the general term "self-interest" is suspect: Iago begins his speech in a declaration of self-interest—"I follow him to serve my turn upon him"—and ends in a declaration of self-division: "I am not what I am." We tend, to be sure, to hear the latter as "I am not what I seem," hence as a simple confirmation of his public deception. But "I am not what I am" goes beyond social feigning: not only does Iago mask himself in society as the honest ancient, but in private he tries out a bewildering succession of brief narratives that critics have attempted, with notorious results, to translate into motives. These inner narratives—shared, that is, only with the audience—continually promise to disclose what lies behind the public deception, to illuminate what Iago calls "the native act and figure" of his heart, and continually fail to do so; or rather, they reveal that his heart is precisely a series of acts and figures, each referring to something else, something just out of our grasp. "I am not what I am" suggests that this elusiveness is permanent, that even self-interest, whose transcendental guarantee is the divine "I am what I am," is a mask. Iago's constant recourse to narrative then is both the affirmation of absolute self-interest and the affirmation of absolute vacancy; the oscillation between the two incompatible positions suggests in Iago the principle of narrativity itself, cut off from original motive and final disclosure. The only termination possible in his case is not revelation but silence.

The question remains why anyone would submit, even unconsciously, to Iago's narrative fashioning. Why would anyone submit to another's narrative at all? For an answer we may recall the pressures on all the figures we have considered in this study and return to our observation that there is a structural resemblance between even a hostile improvisation and its object. In *Othello* the characters have always already experienced submission to narrativity. This is clearest and most important in the case of Othello himself. When Brabantio brings before the Signiory the charge that his daughter has been seduced by witchcraft, Othello promises to deliver "a round unvarnish'd tale . . . / Of my whole course of love" (1.3.90–91), and at the heart of this tale is the telling of tales:

> Her father lov'd me, oft invited me,
> Still question'd me the story of my life,
> From year to year; the battles, sieges, fortunes,
> That I have pass'd:
> I ran it through, even from my boyish days,
> To the very moment that he bade me tell it.
>
> (1.3.128–33)

The telling of the story of one's life—the conception of one's life as a story—is a response to public inquiry: to the demands of the Senate, sitting in judgment or, at the least, to the presence of an inquiring community. When, as recorded in the fourteenth-century documents Le Roy Ladurie has brilliantly studied, the peasants of the Languedoc village of Montaillou are examined by the Inquisition, they respond with a narrative performance: "About 14 years ago, in Lent, towards vespers, I took two sides of salted pork to the house of Guillaume Benet of Montaillou, to have them smoked. There I found Guillemette Benet warming herself by the fire, together with another woman; I put the salted meat in the kitchen and left." And when the Carthaginian queen calls upon her guest to "tell us all things from the first beginning, Grecian guile, your people's trials, and then your journeyings," Aeneas responds, as he must, with a narrative of the destiny decreed by the gods. So too Othello before the Senate or earlier in Brabantio's house responds to questioning with what he calls his "travel's history" or, in the Folio reading, as if noting the genre, his "traveler's history." This history, it should be noted, is not only of events in distant lands and among strange peoples: "I ran it through," Othello declares, from childhood "To the very moment that he bade me tell it." We are on the brink of a Borges-like narrative that is forever constituting itself out of the materials of the present instant, a narrative in which the storyteller is constantly swallowed up by the story. That is, Othello is pressing up against the condition of all discursive representations of identity. He comes dangerously close to recognizing his status as a text, and it is precisely this recognition that the play as a whole will reveal to be insupportable. But, at this point, Othello is still convinced that the text is his own, and he imagines only that he is recounting a lover's performance.

In the forty-fifth sonnet of Sidney's *Astrophil and Stella*, Astrophil complains that while Stella is indifferent to the sufferings she has caused him, she weeps piteous tears at a fable of some unknown lovers. He concludes,

> Then think my dear, that you in me do read
> Of Lovers' ruin some sad Tragedy:
> I am not I, pity the tale of me.

In *Othello* it is Iago who echos that last line—"I am not what I am," the motto of the improviser, the manipulator of signs that bear no resemblance to what they profess to signify—but it is Othello himself who is fully implicated in the situation of the Sidney sonnet: that one can win pity for oneself only by becoming a tale of oneself, and hence by ceasing to be oneself. Of course, Othello thinks that he has triumphed through his narrative self-fashioning:

> she thank'd me,
> And bade me, if I had a friend that lov'd her,
> I should but teach him how to tell my story,
> And that would woo her. Upon this hint I spake:
> She lov'd me for the dangers I had pass'd,
> And I lov'd her that she did pity them.
> (1.3.163–68)

But Iago knows that an identity that has been fashioned as a story can be unfashioned, refashioned, inscribed anew in a different narrative: it is the fate of stories to be consumed or, as we say more politely, interpreted. And even Othello, in his moment of triumph, has a dim intimation of this fate: a half-dozen lines after he has recalled "the Cannibals, that each other eat," he remarks complacently, but with an unmistakable undertone of anxiety, that Desdemona would come "and with a greedy ear / Devour up my discourse" (1.3.149–50).

Paradoxically, in this image of rapacious appetite Othello is recording Desdemona's *submission* to his story, what she calls the consecration of her soul and fortunes "to his honors, and his valiant parts" (1.3.253). What he has both experienced and narrated, she can only embrace as narration:

> my story being done,
> She gave me for my pains a world of sighs;
> She swore i' faith 'twas strange, 'twas passing strange;
> 'Twas pitiful, 'twas wondrous pitiful;

She wish'd she had not heard it, yet she wish'd
That heaven had made her such a man.

(1.3.158–63)

It is, of course, characteristic of early modern culture that male submission to narrative is conceived as active, entailing the fashioning of one's own story (albeit within the prevailing conventions), and female submission as passive, entailing the entrance into marriage in which, to recall Tyndale's definition, the "weak vessel" is put "under the obedience of her husband, to rule her lusts and wanton appetites." As we have seen, Tyndale explains that Sara, "before she was married, was Abraham's sister, and equal with him; but, as soon as she was married, was in subjection, and became without comparison inferior; for so is the nature of wedlock, by the ordinance of God." At least for the world of Renaissance patriarchs, this account is fanciful in its glimpse of an original equality; most women must have entered marriage, like Desdemona, directly from paternal domination. "I do perceive here a divided duty," she tells her father before the Venetian Senate; "you are lord of all my duty,"

but here's my husband:
And so much duty as my mother show'd
To you, preferring you before her father,
So much I challenge, that I may profess,
Due to the Moor my lord.

(1.3.185–89)

She does not question the woman's obligation to obey, invoking instead only the traditional right to transfer her duty. Yet though Desdemona proclaims throughout the play her submission to her husband—"Commend me to my kind lord," she gasps in her dying words—that submission does not accord wholly with the male dream of female passivity. She was, Brabantio tells us,

A maiden never bold of spirit,
So still and quiet, that her motion
Blush'd at her self,

(1.3.94–96)

yet even this self-abnegation in its very extremity unsettles what we may assume was her father's expectation:

So opposite to marriage, that she shunn'd
The wealthy curled darlings of our nation.

(1.2.67–68)

And, of course, her marriage choice is, for Brabantio, an act of astonishing disobedience, explicable only as the somnambulistic behavior of one bewitched or drugged. He views her elopement not as a transfer of obedience but as theft or treason or a reckless escape from what he calls his "guardage." Both he and Iago remind Othello that her marriage suggests not submission but deception:

> She did deceive her father, marrying you;
> And when she seem'd to shake and fear your looks,
> She lov'd them most.
>
> (3.3.210–11)

As the sly reference to Othello's "looks" suggests, the scandal of Desdemona's marriage consists not only in her failure to receive her father's prior consent but in her husband's blackness. That blackness—the sign of all that the society finds frightening and dangerous—is the indelible witness to Othello's permanent status as an outsider, no matter how highly the state may value his services or how sincerely he has embraced its values. The safe passage of the female from father to husband is irreparably disrupted, marked as an escape: "O heaven," Brabantio cries, "how got she out?" (1.1.169).

Desdemona's relation to her lord Othello should, of course, lay to rest any doubts about her proper submission, but it is not only Brabantio's opposition and Othello's blackness that raise such doubts, even in the midst of her intensest declarations of love. There is rather a quality in that love itself that unsettles the orthodox schema of hierarchical obedience and makes Othello perceive her submission to his discourse as a devouring of it. We may perceive this quality most clearly in the exquisite moment of the lovers' reunion on Cyprus:

> OTHELLO: It gives me wonder great as my content
> To see you here before me: O my soul's joy,
> If after every tempest come such calmness,
> May the winds blow, till they have waken'd death,
> And let the labouring bark climb hills of seas,
> Olympus-high, and duck again as low
> As hell's from heaven. If it were now to die,
> 'Twere now to be most happy, for I fear
> My soul hath her content so absolute,
> That not another comfort, like to this
> Succeeds in unknown fate.

DESDEMONA: The heavens forbid
But that our loves and comforts should increase,
Even as our days do grow.
OTHELLO: Amen to that, sweet powers!
I cannot speak enough of this content,
It stops me here, it is too much of joy.
(2.1.183–97)

Christian orthodoxy in both Catholic and Protestant Europe could envision a fervent mutual love between husband and wife, the love expressed most profoundly by Saint Paul in words that are cited and commented upon in virtually every discussion of marriage:

> So men are bound to love their own wives as their own bodies. He that loveth his own wife, loveth himself. For never did any man hate his own flesh, but nourisheth and cherisheth it, even as the Lord doth the congregation: for we are members of his body, of his flesh and of his bones. For this cause shall a man leave father and mother, and shall be joined unto his wife, and they two shall be one flesh. This mystery is great, but I speak of Christ and of the congregation.

Building upon this passage and upon its source in *Genesis*, commentators could write, like the Reformer Thomas Becon, that marriage is a "high, holy, and blessed order of life, ordained not of man, but of God, yea and that not in this sinful world, but in paradise that most joyful garden of pleasure." But like the Pauline text itself, all such discussions of married love begin and end by affirming the larger order of authority and submission within which marriage takes its rightful place. The family, as William Gouge puts it, "is a little Church, and a little Commonwealth . . . whereby trial may be made of such as are fit for any place of authority, or of subjection in Church or Commonwealth."

In Othello's ecstatic words, the proper sentiments of a Christian husband sit alongside something else: a violent oscillation between heaven and hell, a momentary possession of the soul's absolute content, an archaic sense of monumental scale, a dark fear—equally archaic, perhaps—of "unknown fate." Nothing *conflicts* openly with Christian orthodoxy, but the erotic intensity that informs almost every word is experienced in tension with it. This tension is less a manifestation of some atavistic "blackness" specific to Othello than a manifestation of the colonial power of Christian doctrine over sexuality, a power visible at this point precisely in its inherent limitation. That is, we glimpse in this brief moment the *boundary* of the orthodox, the strain of its control, the potential disruption of its hegemony by passion. This scene, let us stress, does not depict rebellion or even complaint—Desdemona invokes "the heavens" and Othello answers, "Amen to that, sweet powers!" Yet the plural here eludes, if only slightly, a serene affirmation of orthodoxy: the powers in their heavens do not refer unmistakably to the Christian God, but rather are the nameless transcendent forces that protect and enhance erotic love. To perceive the difference, we might recall that if Augustine argues, against the gnostics, that God had intended Adam and Eve to procreate in paradise, he insists at the same time that our first parents would have experienced sexual intercourse without the excitement of the flesh. How then could Adam have had an erection? Just as there are persons, Augustine writes, "who can move their ears, either one at a time, or both together" and others who have "such command of their bowels, that they can break wind continuously at pleasure, so as to produce the effect of singing," so, before the Fall, Adam would have had fully rational, willed control of the organ of generation and thus would have needed no erotic arousal. "Without the seductive stimulus of passion, with calmness of mind and with no corrupting of the integrity of the body, the husband would lie upon the bosom of his wife," and in this placid union, the semen could reach the womb "with the integrity of the female genital organ being preserved, just as now, with that same integrity being safe, the menstrual flow of blood can be emitted from the womb of a virgin." Augustine grants that even Adam and Eve, who alone could have done so, failed to experience this "passionless generation," since they were expelled from paradise before they had a chance to try it. Nevertheless, the ideal of Edenic placidity, untried but intended by God for mankind, remains as a reproach to all fallen sexuality, an exposure of its inherent violence.

The rich and disturbing pathos of the lovers' passionate reunion in *Othello* derives then not only from our awareness that Othello's premonition is tragically accurate, but from a rent, a moving ambivalence, in his experience of the ecstatic moment itself. The "calmness" of which he speaks may express gratified desire, but, as the repeated invocation of death suggests, it may equally express the longing for a final *release* from desire, from the dangerous violence, the sense of extremes, the laborious climbing and falling out of control that is experienced in the tempest. To be sure, Othello *welcomes* this tempest, with its charge of erotic feeling, but he does so for the sake of the ultimate consummation that the experience can call into being: "If after every tempest come such calmness . . . ." That which men most fear to look upon in the storm—death—is for

Othello that which makes the storm endurable. If the death he invokes may figure not the release from desire but its fulfillment—for *death* is a common Renaissance term for orgasm—this fulfillment is characteristically poised between an anxious sense of self-dissolution and a craving for decisive closure. If Othello's words suggest an ecstatic acceptance of sexuality, an absolute content, they suggest simultaneously that for him sexuality is a menacing voyage to reach a longed-for heaven; it is one of the dangers to be passed. Othello embraces the erotic as a supreme form of romantic narrative, a tale of risk and violence issuing forth at last in a happy and final tranquility.

Desdemona's response is in an entirely different key:

> The heavens forbid
> But that our loves and comforts should increase,
> Even as our days do grow.

This is spoken to allay Othello's fear, but may it not instead augment it? For if Othello characteristically responds to his experience by shaping it as a story, Desdemona's reply denies the possibility of such narrative control and offers instead a vision of unabating increase. Othello says "Amen" to this vision, but it arouses in him a feeling at once of overflowing and inadequacy:

> I cannot speak enough of this content,
> It stops me here, it is too much of joy.

Desdemona has once again devoured up his discourse, and she has done so precisely in bringing him comfort and content. Rather than simply confirming male authority, her submission eroticizes everything to which it responds, from the "disastrous chances" and "moving accidents" Othello relates, to his simplest demands, to his very mistreatment of her:

> my love doth so approve him,
> That even his stubbornness, his checks and frowns,—
> Prithee unpin me,—have grace and favour in them.
> (4.3.19–21)

The other women in the play, Bianca and Emilia, both have moments of disobedience to the men who possess and abuse them—in the case of Emilia, it is a heroic disobedience for which she pays with her life. Desdemona performs no such acts of defiance, but her erotic submission, conjoined with Iago's murderous cunning, far more effectively, if unintentionally, subverts her husband's carefully fashioned identity.

We will examine more fully the tragic process of this subversion, but it is important to grasp first that Othello's loss of himself—a loss depicted discursively in his incoherent ravings—arises not only from the fatal conjunction of Desdemona's love and Iago's hate, but from the nature of that identity, from what we have called his submission to narrative self-fashioning. We may invoke in this connection Lacan's observation that the source of the subject's frustration in psychoanalysis is ultimately neither the silence nor the reply of the analyst:

> Is it not rather a matter of frustration inherent in the very discourse of the subject? Does the subject not become engaged in an ever-growing dispossession of that being of his, concerning which—by dint of sincere portraits which leave its idea no less incoherent, of rectifications which do not succeed in freeing its essence, of stays and defenses which do not prevent his statue from tottering, of narcissistic embraces which become like a puff of air in animating it—he ends up by recognizing that this being has never been anything more than his construct in the Imaginary and that this construct disappoints all of his certitudes? For in this labor which he undertakes to reconstruct this construct *for another*, he finds again the fundamental alienation which made him construct it *like another one*, and which has always destined it to be stripped from him *by another*.

Shakespeare's military hero, it may be objected, is particularly far removed from this introspective project, a project that would seem, in any case, to have little bearing upon any Renaissance text. Yet I think it is no accident that nearly every phrase of Lacan's critique of psychoanalysis seems a brilliant reading of *Othello*, for I would propose that there is a deep resemblance between the construction of the self in analysis—at least as Lacan conceives it—and Othello's self-fashioning. The resemblance is grounded in the dependence of even the innermost self upon a language that is always necessarily given from without and upon representation before an audience. I do not know if such are the conditions of human identity, apart from its expression in psychoanalysis, but they are unmistakably the conditions of theatrical identity, where existence is conferred upon a character by the playwright's language and the actor's performance. And in *Othello* these governing circumstances of the medium itself are reproduced and intensified in the hero's situation: his identity depends upon a constant performance, as we have seen, of his "story," a loss of his own origins, an embrace and perpetual reiteration of the norms of another culture. It is this dependence that gives Othello, the warrior and alien, a relation to Christian values that is the existential equivalent of a religious vocation; he cannot allow himself the moderately flexible adherence that most ordinary men have toward their own formal beliefs. Christianity is the alienating yet constitutive force in Othello's identity, and if we seek a discursive mode in the play that is the social equivalent of the experience Lacan depicts, we will find it in *confession*. Othello himself invokes before the Venetian Senate the absolute integrity of confession, conceived, it appears, not as the formal auricular rite of penitence but as a generalized self-scrutiny in God's presence:

> as faithful as to heaven
> I do confess the vices of my blood,
> So justly to your grave ears I'll present
> How I did thrive in this fair lady's love,
> And she in mine.
> (1.3.123–36)

The buried identification here between the vices of the blood and mutual thriving in love is fully exhumed by the close of the play when confession has become a virtually obsessional theme. Theological and juridical confession are fused in Othello's mind when, determined first to exact a deathbed confession, he comes to take Desdemona's life:

> If you bethink yourself of any crime,
> Unreconcil'd as yet to heaven and grace,
> Solicit for it straight . . . .
> Therefore confess thee freely of thy sin,
> For to deny each article with oath
> Cannot remove, nor choke the strong conceit,
> That I do groan withal: thou art to die.
> (5.2.26–28, 54–57)

The sin that Othello wishes Desdemona to confess is adultery, and her refusal to do so frustrates the achievement of what in theology was called "a good, complete confession." He feels the outrage of the thwarted system that needs to imagine itself merciful, sacramental, when it disciplines:

> thou dost stone thy heart,
> And makest me call what I intend to do
> A murder, which I thought a sacrifice.
> (5.2.64–66)

We are at last in a position to locate the precise nature of the symbolic structure into which Iago inserts himself in his brilliant improvisation: this structure is the centuries-old Christian doctrine of sexuality, policed socially and psychically, as we have already seen, by confession. To Iago, the Renaissance skeptic, this system has a somewhat archaic ring, as if it were an earlier stage of development which his own modern sensibility had cast off. Like the Lucayan religion to the conquistadors, the orthodox doctrine that governs Othello's sexual attitudes—his simultaneous idealization and mistrust of women—seems to Iago sufficiently close to be recognizable, sufficiently distant to be manipulable. We watch him manipulate it directly at the beginning of act 4, when he leads Othello through a brutally comic parody of the late medieval confessional manuals with their casuistical attempts to define the precise moment at which venial temptation passes over into mortal sin:

> IAGO: To kiss in private?
> OTHELLO: An unauthoriz'd kiss.
> IAGO: Or to be naked with her friend abed,
> An hour, or more, not meaning any harm?
> OTHELLO: Naked abed, Iago, and not mean harm?
> It is hypocrisy against the devil:
> They that mean virtuously, and yet do so,
> The devil their virtue tempts, and they tempt heaven.
> IAGO: So they do nothing, 'tis a venial slip.
> (4.1.2–9)

Iago in effect assumes an extreme version of the laxist position in such manuals in order to impel Othello toward the rigorist version that viewed adultery as one of the most horrible of mortal sins, more detestable, in the words of the *Eruditorium penitentiale*, "than homicide or plunder," and hence formerly deemed punishable, as several authorities remind us, by death. Early Protestantism did not soften this position. Indeed, in the mid-sixteenth century, Tyndale's erstwhile collaborator, George Joye, called for a return to the Old Testament penalty for adulterers. "God's law," he writes, "is to punish adultery with death for the tranquillity and commonwealth of His church." This is not an excessive or vindictive course; on the contrary, "to take away and to cut off putrified and corrupt members from the whole body, lest they poison and destroy the body, is the law of love." When Christian magistrates leave adultery unpunished, they invite more betrayals and risk the ruin of the realm, for as Protestants in particular repeatedly observe, the family is an essential component of an interlocking social and theological network. Hence adultery is a sin with the gravest of repercussions; in the words of the great Cambridge Puritan William Perkins, it "destroyeth the Seminary of the Church, which is *a godly seed* in the family, and it breaketh the covenant between the parties and God; it robs another of the precious ornament of chastity, which is a gift of the Holy Ghost; it dishonors their bodies and maketh them temples of the devil; and the Adulterer maketh his family a Stews." It is in the bitter spirit of these convictions that Othello enacts the grotesque comedy of treating his wife as a strumpet and the tragedy of executing her in the name of justice, lest she betray more men.

But we still must ask how Iago manages to persuade Othello that Desdemona has committed adultery, for all of the cheap tricks Iago plays seem somehow inadequate to produce the unshakable conviction of his wife's defilement that seizes Othello's soul and drives him mad. After all, as Iago taunts Othello, he cannot achieve the point of vantage of God whom the Venetian women let "see the pranks / They dare not show their husbands" (3.3.206–7):

> Would you, the supervisor, grossly gape on,
> Behold her topp'd?
>
> (3.3.401–2)

How then, without "ocular proof" and in the face of both love and common sense, is Othello so thoroughly persuaded? To answer this, we must recall the syntactic ambiguity we noted earlier—"to abuse Othello's ear, / That he is too familiar with his wife"—and turn to a still darker aspect of orthodox Christian doctrine, an aspect central both to the confessional system and to Protestant self-scrutiny. *Omnis amator feruentior est adulter*, goes the Stoic epigram, and Saint Jerome does not hesitate to draw the inevitable inference: "An adulterer is he who is too ardent a lover of his wife." Jerome quotes Seneca: "All love of another's wife is shameful; so too, too much love of your own. A wise man ought to love his wife with judgment, not affection. Let him control his impulses and not be borne headlong into copulation. Nothing is fouler than to love a wife like an adultress. . . . Let them show themselves to their wives not as lovers, but as husbands." The words echo through more than a thousand years of Christian writing on marriage, and, in the decisive form given them by Augustine and his commentators, remain essentially unchallenged by the leading continental Reformers of the sixteenth and early seventeenth century, by Tudor ecclesiastical authorities, and even by Elizabethan and Jacobean Puritans who sharply opposed so many conservative Anglican doctrines. There is, to be sure, in all shades of Protestantism an attack on the Catholic doctrine of celibacy and a celebration of married love, a celebration that includes acknowledgment of the legitimate role of sexual pleasure. But for Reformer as for Catholic, this acknowledgment is hedged about with warnings and restrictions. The "man who shows no modesty or comeliness in conjugal intercourse," writes Calvin, "is committing adultery with his wife," and the *King's Book*, attributed to Henry VIII, informs its readers that in lawful matrimony a man may break the Seventh Commandment "and live unchaste with his own wife, if he do unmeasurably or inordinately serve his or her fleshly appetite or lust."

In the Augustinian conception, as elaborated by Raymond of Peñaforte, William of Rennes, and others, there are four motives for conjugal intercourse: to conceive offspring; to render the marital debt to one's partner so that he or she might avoid incontinency; to avoid fornication oneself; and to satisfy desire. The first two motives are without sin and excuse intercourse; the third is a venial sin; the fourth—to satisfy desire—is mortal. Among the many causes that underlie this institutional hostility to desire is the tenacious existence, in various forms, of the belief that pleasure constitutes a legitimate release from dogma and constraint. Thus when asked by the Inquisition about her happy past liaison with the heretical priest of Montaillou, the young Grazide Lizier replies with naive frankness, "in those days it pleased me, and it pleased the priest, that he should know me carnally, and be known by me; and so I did not think I was sinning, and neither did he." "With Pierre Clergue," she explains, "I liked it. And so it could not displease God. It was not a sin." For the peasant girl, apparently, pleasure was the guarantee of innocence: "But now, with him, it does not please me any more. And so now, if he knew me carnally, I should think it a sin." A comparable attitude, derived not from peasant culture but from the troubadours, evidently lies behind the more sophisticated courtship of Romeo: "Thus from my lips, by thine my sin is purged."

It should not surprise us that churchmen, Catholic and Protestant alike, would seek to crush such dangerous notions, nor that they would extend their surveillance and discipline to married couples and warn that excessive pleasure in the marriage bed is at least a potential violation of the Seventh Commandment. "Nothing is more vile," says Raymond's influential *summa*, "than to love your wife in adulterous fashion." The conjugal act may be without sin, writes the rigorist Nicolaus of Ausimo, but only if "in the performance of this act there is no enjoyment of pleasure." Few *summas* and no marriage manuals take so extreme a position, but virtually all are in agreement that the active *pursuit* of pleasure in sexuality is damnable, for as Jacobus Ungarelli writes in the sixteenth century, those who undertake intercourse for pleasure "exclude God from their minds, act as brute beasts, lack reason, and if they begin marriage for this reason, are given over to the power of the devil."

Confessors then must determine if the married penitent has a legitimate excuse for intercourse and if the act has been performed with due regard for "matrimonial chastity," while Protestants who have rejected auricular confession must similarly scrutinize their own behavior for signs that their pleasure has been too "spacious." "Lust is more spacious than love," writes Alexander Niccoles in the early seventeenth century; it "hath no mean, no bound . . . more deep, more dangerous than the Sea, and less restrained, for the Sea hath bounds, but it [lust] hath none." Such unbounded love is a kind of idolatry, an encroachment upon a Christian's debt of loving obedience to God, and it ultimately destroys the marital relationship as well. Immoderate love, another Puritan divine warns, "will either be blown down by some storm or tempest of displeasure, or fall of itself, or else degenerate into jealousy, the most devouring and fretting canker that can harbor in a married person's breast."

These anxieties, rich in implication for *Othello*, are frequently tempered in Protestant writings by a recognition of the joyful ardor of young married couples, but there remains a constant fear of excess, and, as Ambrose observed centuries earlier, even the most plausible excuse for sexual passion is shameful in the old: "Youths generally assert the desire for generation. How much more shameful for the old to do what is shameful for the young to confess." Othello himself seems eager to ward off this shame; he denies before the Senate that he seeks

> To please the palate of my appetite,
> Nor to comply with heat, the young affects
> In me defunct.
>
> (1.3.262–64)

But Desdemona makes no such disclaimer; indeed her declaration of passion is frankly, though by no means exclusively, sexual:

> That I did love the Moor, to live with him,
> My downright violence, and scorn of fortunes,
> May trumpet to the world: my heart's subdued
> Even to the utmost pleasure of my lord.
>
> (1.3.248–51)

This moment of erotic intensity, this frank acceptance of pleasure and submission to her spouse's pleasure, is, I would argue, as much as Iago's slander the cause of Desdemona's death, for it awakens the deep current of sexual anxiety in Othello, anxiety that with Iago's help expresses itself in quite orthodox fashion as the perception of adultery. Othello unleashes upon Cassio—"Michael Cassio, / That came a-wooing with you" (3.3.71–72)—the fear of pollution, defilement, brutish violence that is bound up with his own experience of sexual pleasure, while he must destroy Desdemona both for her excessive experience of pleasure and for awakening such sensations in himself. Like Guyon in the Bower of Bliss, Othello transforms his complicity in erotic excess and his fear of engulfment into a "purifying," saving violence:

> Like to the Pontic sea,
> Whose icy current and compulsive course
> Ne'er feels retiring ebb, but keeps due on
> To the Propontic and the Hellespont,
> Even so my bloody thoughts, with violent pace,
> Shall ne'er look back, ne'er ebb to humble love,
> Till that a capable and wide revenge
> Swallow them up.
> (3.3.460–67)

His insupportable sexual experience has been, as it were, displaced and absorbed by the act of revenge which can swallow up not only the guilty lovers but—as the syntax suggests—his own "bloody thoughts."

Such is the achievement of Iago's improvisation on the religious sexual doctrine in which Othello believes; true to that doctrine, pleasure itself becomes for Othello pollution, a defilement of his property in Desdemona and in himself. It is at the level of this dark, sexual revulsion that Iago has access to Othello, access assured, as we should expect, by the fact that beneath his cynical modernity and professed self-love Iago reproduces in himself the same psychic structure. He is as intensely preoccupied with adultery, while his anxiety about his own sexuality may be gauged from the fact that he conceives his very invention, as the images of engendering suggest, as a kind of demonic semen that will bring forth monsters. Indeed Iago's discourse—his assaults on women, on the irrationality of eros, on the brutishness of the sexual act—reiterates virtually to the letter the orthodox terms of Ungarelli's attack on those who seek pleasure in intercourse.

The improvisational process we have been discussing depends for its success upon the concealment of its symbolic center, but as the end approaches this center becomes increasingly visible. When, approaching the marriage bed on which Desdemona has spread the wedding sheets, Othello rages, "Thy bed, lust stain'd, shall with lust's blood be spotted" (5.1.36), he comes close to revealing his tormenting identification of marital sexuality—limited perhaps to the night he took Desdemona's virginity—and adultery. The orthodox element of this identification is directly observed—

> this sorrow's heavenly,
> It strikes when it does love—
> (5.2.21–22)

and on her marriage bed / deathbed Desdemona seems at last to pluck out the heart of the mystery:

> OTHELLO: Think on thy sins.
> DESDEMONA: They are loves I bear to you.
> OTHELLO: And for that thou diest.
> DESDEMONA: That death's unnatural, that kills for loving.
> (5.2.39–42)

The play reveals at this point not the unfathomable darkness of human motives but their terrible transparency, and the horror of the revelation is its utter inability to deflect violence. Othello's identity is entirely caught up in the narrative structure that drives him to turn Desdemona into a being incapable of pleasure, a piece of "monumental alabaster," so that he will at last be able to love her without the taint of adultery:

> Be thus, when thou art dead, and I will kill thee,
> And love thee after.
> (5.2.18–19)

It is as if Othello had found in a necrophilic fantasy the secret solution to the intolerable demands of the rigorist sexual ethic, and the revelation that Cassio has not slept with Desdemona leads only to a doubling of this solution, for the adulterous sexual pleasure that Othello had projected upon his lieutenant now rebounds upon himself. Even with the exposure of Iago's treachery, then, there is for Othello no escape—rather a still deeper submission to narrative, a reaffirmation of the self as story, but now split suicidally between the defender of the faith and the circumcised enemy who must be destroyed. Lodovico's bizarrely punning response to Othello's final speech—"O bloody period!"—insists precisely upon the fact that it was a speech, that this life fashioned as a text is ended as a text.

To an envious contemporary like Robert Greene, Shakespeare seems a kind of green-room Iago, appropriating for himself the labors of others. In *Othello* Shakespeare seems to acknowledge, represent, and explore his affinity to the malicious improviser, but, of course, his relation to the theater and to his culture is far more complex than such an affinity could suggest. There are characters in his works who can improvise without tragic results, characters who can embrace a mobility of desire—one of whose emblems is the male actor playing a female character dressed up as a male—that neither Iago, nor Othello, nor Desdemona can endure. Destructive violence is not Shakespeare's only version of these materials, and even in *Othello*, Iago is not the playwright's only representation of himself. Still, at the least we must grant Robert Greene that it would have seemed fatal to be imitated by Shakespeare. He possessed a limitless talent for entering into the consciousness of another, perceiving its deepest structures as a manipulable fiction, reinscribing it into his own narrative form. If in the late plays, he experiments with controlled disruptions of narrative, moments of eddying and ecstasy, these invariably give way to reaffirmations of self-fashioning through story.

Montaigne, who shares many of Shakespeare's most radical perceptions, invents in effect a brilliant mode of *nonnarrative* self-fashioning: "I cannot keep my subject still. It goes along befuddled and staggering, with a natural drunkenness. I take it in this condition, just as it is at the moment I give my attention to it." Shakespeare by contrast remains throughout his career the supreme purveyor of "empathy," the fashioner of narrative selves, the master improviser. Where Montaigne withdrew to his study, Shakespeare became the presiding genius of a popular, urban art form with the capacity to foster psychic mobility in the service of Elizabethan power; he became the principal maker of what we may see as the prototype of the mass media Professor Lerner so admires.

Finally, we may ask, is this service to power a function of the theater itself or of Shakespeare's relation to his medium? The answer, predictably, is both. The theater is widely perceived in the period as the concrete manifestation of the histrionic quality of life, and, more specifically, of power—the power of the prince who stands as an actor upon a stage before the eyes of the nation, the power of God who enacts His will in the Theater of the World. The stage justifies itself against recurrent charges of immorality by invoking this normative function: it is the expression of those rules that govern a properly ordered society and displays visibly the punishment, in laughter and violence, that is meted out upon those who violate the rules. Most playwrights pay at least professional homage to these values; they honor the institutions that enable them to earn their keep and give voice to the ideology that holds together both their "mystery" and the society at large.

In Marlowe, as we have seen [elsewhere], we encounter a playwright at odds with this ideology. If the theater normally reflects and flatters the royal sense of itself as national performance, Marlowe struggles to expose the underlying motives of any performance of power. If the theater normally affirms God's providence, Marlowe explores the tragic needs and interests that are served by all such affirmations. If the Elizabethan stage functions as one of the public uses of spectacle to impose normative ethical patterns on the urban masses, Marlowe enacts a relentless challenge to those patterns and undermines employment of rhetoric and violence in their service.

Shakespeare approaches his culture not, like Marlowe, as rebel and blasphemer, but rather as dutiful servant, content to improvise a part of his own within its orthodoxy. And if after centuries, that improvisation has been revealed to us as embodying an almost boundless challenge to the culture's every tenet, a devastation of every source, the author of *Othello* would have understood that such a revelation scarcely matters. After all, the heart of a successful improvisation lies in concealment, not exposure; and besides, as we have seen, even a hostile improvisation reproduces the relations of power that it hopes to displace and absorb. This is not to dismiss the power of hatred or the significance of distinctions—it matters a great deal whether Othello or Iago, the Lucayans or the Spaniards prevail—only to suggest the boundaries that define the possibility of any improvisational contact, even contact characterized by hidden malice.

I would not want to argue, in any event, that Shakespeare's relation to his culture is defined by hidden malice. Such a case can no doubt be made for many of the plays—stranger things have been said—but it will sound forced and unconvincing, just as the case for Shakespeare as an unwavering, unquestioning apologist for Tudor ideology sounds forced and unconvincing. The solution here is not, I suggest, that the truth lies somewhere in between. Rather the truth itself is radically unstable and yet constantly stabilized, as unstable as those male authorities that affirm themselves only to be undermined by subversive women and then to be reconstituted in a different guise. If any reductive generalization about Shakespeare's relation to his culture seems dubious, it is because his plays offer no single timeless affirmation or denial of legitimate authority and no central, unwavering authorial presence. Shakespeare's language and themes are caught up, like the medium itself, in unsettling repetitions, committed to the shifting voices and audiences, with their shifting aesthetic assumptions and historical imperatives, that govern a living theater.

Criticism can legitimately show—as I hope my discussion of *Othello* does—that Shakespeare relentlessly *explores* the relations of power in a given culture. That more than exploration is involved is much harder to demonstrate convincingly. If there are intimations in Shakespeare of a release from the complex narrative orders in which everyone is inscribed, these intimations do not arise from bristling resistance or strident denunciation—the mood of a Jaques or Timon. They arise paradoxically from a peculiarly intense *submission* whose downright violence undermines everything it was meant to shore up, the submission depicted not in Othello or Iago but in Desdemona. As both the play and its culture suggest, the arousal of intense, purposeless pleasure is only superficially a confirmation of existing values, established selves. In Shakespeare's narrative art, liberation from the massive power structures that determine social and psychic reality is glimpsed in an *excessive* aesthetic delight, an erotic embrace of those very structures—the embrace of a Desdemona whose love is more deeply unsettling than even a Iago's empathy.

# Othello's Occupation: Shakespeare and the Romance of Chivalry

*Mark Rose*

O now, for ever
Farewell the tranquil mind! farewell content!
Farewell the plumed troops, and the big wars
That makes ambition virtue! O, farewell!
Farewell the neighing steed and the shrill trump,
The spirit-stirring drum, th' ear-piercing fife,
The royal banner, and all quality,
Pride, pomp, and circumstance of glorious war!
And O you mortal engines, whose rude throats
Th' immortal Jove's dread clamors counterfeit,
Farewell! Othello's occupation's gone.
(*Othello*, 3.3.347–57)

Othello's adieus to tranquility and content at the start of this speech evoke something more like the pastoral than the military ideal. Even when the imagery becomes explicitly military in the evocation of the "plumed troops" and the "big wars" there is a subtle continuity with the opening pastoralism. Here the lines suggest a transformation in which "ambition," which is a vice in a world defined by pastoral content, becomes a "virtue" in a martial context—that is, both a positive good, and in the archaic sense of *virtu*, a source of strength. Moreover, the static quality of "plumed troops" and "big wars" is compatible with the feeling the lines convey that

From *English Literary Renaissance* 15, no. 3 (Autumn 1985). © 1985 by *English Literary Renaissance*.

something like pastoral *otium* is being continued in a martial vein. Explicit activity enters the picture when Othello imagines the world he has lost as a parade of neighing horses and playing instruments—trumpet, drum, and fife—an ascending procession of sound that climaxes in the godlike roar of the cannon. "Farewell! Othello's occupation's gone." Six times in eleven lines Othello says farewell. The repetition articulates the speech, contributing to the sense of a procession passing with Othello bidding adieu to each of the squadrons in the parade of his life. It also unifies the speech, turning it into a nostalgic lament for a paradoxically apprehended martial pastoral.

What has Othello lost? The contradictions in this speech, at once static and active, pastoral and martial, convey the emotional urgency with which an image of the perfected world of absolute being is here fashioned. It is a world in which everything, including the neighing of horses and the booming of cannon, takes on the aspect of music; a world without stress, one in which even ambitious striving for glory has been reconceived as a form of tranquility. To participate in the harmonious clamor of this grand march in which mortal engines counterfeit the huge sounds of immortal Jove is to live at the farthest verge of human possibility. It is to be nearly as absolute as a god. Plainly such a state of being, one in which there is no gap between desire and satisfaction, between, as Macbeth puts it, the firstlings of the heart and the firstlings of the hand, is a condition radically incompatible with self-reflection, thought, or uncertainty of any kind. To banish Othello from such an Eden, proof of Desdemona's infidelity is unnecessary; mere suspicion will do as well as certainty.

Why should suspicion of Desdemona's infidelity end Othello's occupation as a soldier? It helps to observe that Othello conceives himself in this speech as a type of the knight validated by the absolute worthiness of the mistress he serves. Call the mistress into question and not only the knight's activity but his very identity collapses. Of course in this case the mistress, the necessarily unattainable lady of romance, has become the wife: sexual availability—as opposed to the intensity of mere fantasizing—has entered the picture. Even without Iago's machinations, then, the romantic image of the absolute worthiness of the lady is at best unstable. Others have developed this aspect of Othello's vulnerability to Iago. Here let us note simply that this speech is a clue to Othello's romanticizing imagination. It is a piece with his address to the Senate in which he retells the story of his adventures among cannibals and monsters, his speech to Desdemona about the magic in the web of the handkerchief in which he invokes witches and charms as a way of explaining its overwhelming significance, or his final speech in which he recalls the exotic turbaned Turk in order to explain why he is about to slay himself. One might interpret *Othello* as a kind of tragic *Don Quixote,* a play in which Shakespeare explores the ways in which a romanticizing imagination can lead to devastating error. Yet despite the appeal of such an approach—and certainly it would be illuminating up to a point—we should note that Othello's romanticism is neither so explicit as Don Quixote's nor so firmly demarcated from the general world of the narrative.

There are no giants or dragons in *Othello.* The play's military world consists of generals, lieutenants, and ancients rather than knights, squires, evil magicians, and faithless Saracens. It is a world in which career advancement can be presented as a plausible motive for action; it is a comparatively workaday place of fleets, intelligence reports, and expeditionary forces. But the proximate realism should not blind us to the play's romantic aspects. There are Christian soldiers and threatening infidels here. Othello, a black warrior of royal lineage who turns out to be capable of astonishing violence, has something of a Savage Knight about him, and Desdemona may well in the constancy of her affection recall a Princess of Love and Chastity. Iago is no magician—indeed, he explicitly denies that he works by witchcraft—and yet his ensnarement of Othello's soul together with his manipulation of his perceptions may recall Spenser's Archimago, who similarly provides Redcross with ocular proof of his lady's infidelity. Moreover, all these elements reminiscent of chivalric romance—Othello's royal blood and adventurous past, the somewhat miraculous quality of Desdemona's innocence, the air of diabolical mystery that clings to Iago, the background of war with the infidel—are Shakespeare's additions to the Othello story as he found it in Cinthio's novella. Not just Othello's imagination but, I would suggest, Shakespeare's own is informed by the patterns of chivalric romance.

## II

A few words about the Elizabethan chivalric revival are in order here. As Roy Strong says, "It is one of the great paradoxes of the Elizabethan world, one of its touchstones, that an age of social, political and religious revolution should cling to and deliberately erect a façade of the trappings of feudalism." Elizabethan culture was saturated with feudal idealism. In life and in art chivalric themes were pervasive. By the 1580s the spectacular Accession Day Tilts had reached their fully developed form. In this period, too, Robert Smythson was designing such fantasy castles as Wollaton Hall, Sidney was writing the *Arcadia,* Spenser was writing *The Faerie Queene,* and the London stages were populated by damsels in distress, knights in armor, and wicked enchanters in dozens of plays—most now lost—with names like *Herpetulus the Blue Knight and Perobia, The History of the Solitary Knight*, and *Sir Clyomon and Sir Clamydes*. Chivalric fantasies of service to the Virgin Queen shaped Elizabethan court style and also affected foreign policy. One product of the chivalric revival was Sidney's *Arcadia*, another was his death in 1586 in a campaign in which romantic notions continually obscured for Eliza's knights the complex facts of a situation in which Dutch burghers were attempting to throw off Spanish rule.

Northrop Frye's conception of romance as "the search of the libido or desiring self for a fulfillment that will deliver it from the anxieties of reality but will still contain that reality" might well be a gloss on the Elizabethan effort to turn reality into a romance. The late sixteenth century was a time of dramatic social changes and probably also a period of considerable social anxiety. London was burgeoning, commerce was developing rapidly, old bonds of service and obligation were yielding to new relationships based on the marketplace, and the religious unity of Europe was gone forever. Chivalric games and ceremonies helped to obscure the relative newness of so many of the noble families as well as the fact that, despite the continuing prestige of war, the aristocracy had ceased to be a warrior class and was becoming an administrative elite. By this period, as Lawrence Stone has shown, there was little that was particularly feudal about the English nobility, who from an early time had been deeply engaged in entrepreneurial activity. On the other hand, there was little that was clearly bourgeois—in the modern sense—about the sensibility of the Elizabethan middle class. Interestingly, the bourgeois hero tales of the 1590s and early 1600s—Deloney's *Jack of Newbury*, Dekker's *Shoemaker's Holiday* and other stories and plays celebrating the virtues of the new men of commerce—show middle-class figures in feudal postures, fighting and feasting like knights. The usual aspiration of the successful businessman was not to oppose the interests of the landed aristocracy and gentry but to join them as soon as possible, one notable case in point being Shakespeare himself.

The chivalric revival assimilated the complexities of the present to a mythical world of the past, but at its center was the living Queen. In her own person Elizabeth held the contradictions of her culture together, and she did this in part by turning herself into a character, Gloriana, and her life and that of her country into a story. But the moment of magical balance was necessarily brief. By the late 1590s the fervor of the previous decade was gone. Corruption at court was more marked and commented on, and it had become increasingly more difficult for the Queen, who was now a full generation older than her principal courtiers, to play the role of the virginal beauty. Nor should the traumatic effect of the Earl of Essex's rebellion and execution be underestimated. Essex, who is one of the very few contemporary figures to whom Shakespeare directly alludes, was the inheritor of Philip Sidney's sword and of his position in the national imagination as the embodiment of chivalry. According to his biographer, his rise and sudden fall in 1601 probably affected the nation more deeply than any event since the defeat of the Spanish Armada. In any case, the time came when the Elizabethan romances—both the romance enacted by the Queen and those composed by her poets and dramatists—could no longer carry conviction. Despite a brief revival of some of its themes in 1610–1612 at the court of Prince Henry, nothing like the special quality of Elizabethan chivalry could occur again.

## III

I know of no general study of Shakespeare's relation to the romance dramas of the 1570s and 1580s and to the Elizabethan chivalric revival. Nevertheless, it is not hard to see how, for instance, *1 Henry VI* with its opposition between the heroic knight Talbot and the wicked enchantress Joan represents a continuation and transformation of chivalric romance materials, or how similar materials influence the romantic comedies with their disguised and wandering heroines. Moreover, the theme of both historical tetralogies is the disintegration of an absolute world of chivalry, and in this theme the histories might be said to look forward to Othello's farewell to arms. Thus the first tetralogy begins with Henry V's funeral, a symbolic procession that suggests the death of chivalry itself, after which the *Henry VI* plays trace the collapse of the heroic society into faction and civil war. There follows the emergence of Richard the Third, a monstrous antitype of the chivalric hero, and finally the return of chivalry in the person of the Earl of Richmond. The pattern of the second tetralogy is similar. Here the interrupted combat at the start of *Richard II* establishes the lost world of perfected chivalric kingship, after which the plays trace a decline into strife and rebellion and finally the emergence of a new chivalric figure, Prince Hal as Henry V. But this time, we note, the chivalric return is not simply a return. Hal's chivalry is political and contingent rather than mystical and absolute in the vein of Richmond at the end of *Richard III*. Like Elizabeth holding the contradictions of her culture together in her person, Hal holds the contradictions of his history-play world together, and, like her, he does it through self-conscious role-playing.

The tone of Shakespeare's treatment of chivalric themes, like so much else, changes in the early seventeenth century. *Troilus and Cressida*, probably written the year after the Essex rebellion, is biting in its exposure of the putrefied core that seems to hide within the goodly armor of chivalric pretentions, and in *King Lear* not even the spectacular romance-like triumph of the unknown knight Edgar over his evil brother Edmund can prevent the ugly hanging of Cordelia and the play's tragic end. Particularly relevant to *Othello,* however, is the tragedy that immediately precedes it chronologically. It would be hard, I think, to overemphasize the importance of chivalry to *Hamlet.* The play takes its point of departure, and finds its image of the lost chivalric world, in Horatio's evocation of King Hamlet and King Fortinbras locked in a valiant single combat ratified by law and chivalry. It is this evocation of heroic combat in a past time when things were absolutely what they seemed to be that gives meaning to the great falling off that constitutes the play's present world. In creeping into the garden to poison his brother, Claudius has in effect poisoned chivalry. His secret duel with Hamlet, fought with such human weapons as Polonius, Rosencrantz and Guildenstern, and the actors, represents a travesty of chivalric ideals, and the play moves not toward the heroic restorations of the histories but toward a grotesque and deadly recapitulation of the original combat between the kings in Hamlet and Laertes's duel with the poisoned foils, overseen by Osric as chivalric judge-at-arms.

## IV

"I'll pour this pestilence into his ear" (2.3.356) [All citations of Shakespeare refer to *The Riverside Shakespeare,* ed. G. Blakemore Evans]: the language with which Iago introduces his plan for undoing Othello strikingly recalls Claudius's poison poured into the porches of King Hamlet's ears. We can note, too, that Othello's farewell to arms figures in the play's structure in a manner analogous to the image of the kings in combat, providing in its martial pastoral a point of reference against which the present situation, Othello in the agonies of Iago's poison, is to be measured. But the fact that in *Othello* the nostalgic reference point comes in the middle rather than at the start of the tragedy is important; whereas in *Hamlet* chivalry is dead before the play begins, in *Othello* we observe the process of the poisonous transformation. In fact we do more than observe, we participate. In *Hamlet* the audience's representative, the figure who draws us into dramatic engagement with his purposes, is the prince, and Claudius, as his antagonist, becomes in consequence a relatively opaque figure. In *Othello,* as in *Richard III* and *Macbeth,* Shakespeare plays the dynamics of theatrical engagement against moral judgment, and this is one reason that *Othello* does not lapse into melodrama. From the opening in which Iago manipulates Roderigo and Brabantio, the play is structured so that we enter the action from Iago's point of view, and his many strategically placed soliloquies and asides confirm our dramatic engagement with him through at least the first half of the play. Othello himself is magnificent, a commanding and dominating figure, but until the temptation scene and the start of his falling off he is also, like Claudius, apprehended at a certain distance, observed as one might observe a public figure and a stranger.

Othello, the exotic black man from Africa, is a stranger in another, more literal, sense as well. In *Hamlet* and in the history plays the representatives of chivalric perfection—King Hamlet, Henry V in the first tetralogy, Edward the Black Prince as he is evoked at the start of the second tetralogy—are generally ancestral figures. Even the Earl of Richmond and Henry V in the second tetralogy are ancestral figures to the audience if not to the characters in the plays. In *Othello,* however, the knightly defender of Christian civilization is projected as an alien. Othello's blackness is the index of a different orientation toward the chivalric figure. Moreover, as many critics since Bradley have remarked, Iago is a kind of playwright, an artist carefully maneuvering his characters into position to bring his tragedy to fulfillment. Perhaps, then, we can think of *Othello* as a play in which Shakespeare is recapitulating his own earlier representations of an absolute world of chivalry, alienating them, and through Iago representing something like his own role in plotting the disintegration of the absolute world.

## V

> Put money in thy purse . . . I say put money in thy purse . . .
> put money in thy purse . . . put but money in thy purse . . .
> fill thy purse with money . . . put money in thy purse . . .
> Make all the money thou canst . . . therefore make money . . .
> go make money . . . go, provide thy money . . . put money
> enough in your purse.
>
> (1.3.339–81)

It is more than a little tempting to think of Iago as an embodiment of the prodigious energies of the new commercialism of the Renaissance, and thus to turn *Othello* into an allegory in which bourgeois man destroys the representative of the older feudal values. Thus, whereas Othello speaks of the plumed troop and the royal banner in terms that evoke an activity of transcendent worth, Iago can talk casually of "the trade of war" (1.2.1). Iago's speech is shot through with the language of commerce. "I know my price," he says when he describes being passed over for promotion, "I am worth no worse a place" (1.1.11), and, contrasting himself with Cassio, he dismisses the lieutenant as a mere accountant, a "debitor and creditor," and a "counter-caster" (1.1.31). Yet even though he has money and purses on his mind, Iago's motive for bringing down Othello is certainly not profit. Moreover, Othello too can speak in commercial terms, as when he invites Desdemona to bed after their arrival in Cyprus: "Come, my dear love, / The purchase made, the fruits are to ensue; / The profit's yet to come 'tween me and you" (2.3.8–10).

To reduce *Othello* to historical allegory would plainly be to distort the play. Such a reduction would also be anachronistic. As Lawrence Stone and other social historians have taught us, we must beware of imagining anything like a clear-cut opposition in this period between a declining feudal class and a rising bourgeoisie. The late sixteenth and early seventeenth centuries were a time of transition and contradiction, a period in which fundamentally incompatible social forms and structures of thought sat uneasily side by side in a manner that may make us think of those sixteenth-century account books kept partly in Arabic, partly in Roman numerals. An old world of traditional forms and values was largely gone, but a new one had not yet clearly taken shape.

Particularly apparent were the tensions between the traditional feudal values of honor, loyalty, and service, and the less absolute imperatives of the marketplace. On the one hand honor might be regarded as a kind of religion, something worth dying for, as for instance when Cassio equates his good name with his soul: "Reputation, reputation, reputation! O, I have lost my reputation! I have lost the immortal part of myself, and what remains is bestial" (2.3.262–64). On the other, it was often treated as merchandise. "I would to God thou and I knew where a commodity of good names were to be bought," Falstaff says mockingly to Hal (*1 Henry IV*, 1.2.82–83), and a few years later in the Jacobean debasement of honors, good names were openly traded like stocks and bonds. Thus Stone reports that in 1606 Lionel Cranfield bought the making of six knights from his friend Arthur Ingram for £373.1s.8d. In this transitional moment, no simple antithesis between the values of the marketplace and those of the field of honor is possible. Despite his skepticism about honor, Sir John Falstaff is not a bourgeois figure. Likewise, Antonio, the paragon of lordly generosity who is contrasted with Shylock in *The Merchant of Venice,* is not, as we might suppose given the values that he embodies, a feudal figure. Perhaps, then, we should imagine the tension between feudal and commercial codes at this time as less like a modern class struggle than like a medieval psychomachia—that is, as a still internalized struggle in which members of the same group, or even at times a single individual, can be found operating inconsistently, now according to one set of values, now according to another.

The mediation of contradiction can be understood as one of the functions of drama or even of narrative generally. With this in mind let us briefly note that Shakespeare often plays romantic and absolute attitudes against contingent and commercial ones, building drama out of the tension. *The Merchant of Venice* is an obvious case in point, as is *As You Like It* where the absoluteness of Orlando's professions of love is measured against the more mundane view evoked in Rosalind's mockery of dying for love and her advice to Phoebe, "Sell when you can, you are not for all markets" (3.5.60). And yet for all her mockery, Rosalind is, we know, a very romantic young lady, many fathoms deep in love. Just so *1 Henry IV,* in which the romanticism is expressed in chivalric rather than erotic terms, measures Hotspur against Falstaff. Like Rosalind, Hal is able to play both mocker and romantic, or, to make the point at the level of diction where it may be easiest to observe, he is able to blend the language of commerce with that of chivalry, as when he predicts his triumph over Hotspur:

> Percy is but my factor, good my lord,
> To engross up glorious deeds on my behalf;
> And I will call him to so strict account
> That he shall render every glory up,
> Yea, even the slightest worship of his time,
> Or I will tear the reckoning from his heart.
> (3.2.147–52)

In this way the flexibility of language allows contrary systems of value to be expressed. At the same time, the conventions of narrative achieve forward thrust. No practical resolution of the cultural contradiction may be possible but at least there can be the satisfactions of the achievement of narrative closure. In any case, *Othello,* too, incorporates the tension between romantic absolutism and the antithetical values of the marketplace, but here instead of being held in triumphant balance in the style of the 1590s, the brutal power latent in the contradiction is used to drive a tragedy.

## VI

Let us begin by observing a major change that Shakespeare makes in the structure of Cinthio's narrative. In the novella the wicked ensign's revenge is not directed at the Moor so much as at the lady. Cinthio's ensign is a rebuffed suitor whose passion for Desdemona turns to hate. Shakespeare, however, pits Iago directly against Othello. One effect of this change is to obscure the villain's motive. Another is to alter the lady's position in the narrative structure, demoting her from one of the two ultimate figures in the story to an intermediary. Like the handkerchief with which she is associated, Desdemona becomes a kind of object, an instrument of Iago's revenge against Othello. Passed first from Brabantio's hands into the Moor's and then ignorantly thrown away, Shakespeare's Desdemona figures in the narrative as property. Iago's revenge looks forward to the bourgeois style of a later age; he achieves satisfaction by depriving his enemy of his most valued possession.

At the same time that Shakespeare's narrative demotes Desdemona from a person to property, it also elevates her to an angel. Cinthio's lady is a rather matter-of-fact heroine, but Shakespeare's is a transcendent figure who refracts the long series of divine ladies that reaches back through the sonnet and romance heroines of the sixteenth century to, among others, Petrarch's Laura and Dante's Beatrice. Her conversation with Emilia about women who betray their husbands evokes the realm of the marketplace precisely in order to separate her from it absolutely. "Wouldst thou do such a deed for all the world?" she asks Emilia, who replies less romantically that while she would not do it for anything trivial such as a ring or a dress, she certainly would do it for the world: "The world's a huge thing; it is a great price / For a small vice" (4.3.67–69). Later, guiltlessly dying, Desdemona refuses to blame Othello for anything: "Commend me to my kind lord. O, farewell!" (5.2.125). At once property and an angel of selflessness, Desdemona, too, looks forward to the bourgeois age and to its conception of woman.

Behind the contradictions implicit in Shakespeare's Desdemona may be glimpsed the tensions of a moment of cultural transformation. In a penetrating observation, Kenneth Burke suggests that *Othello* incorporates an analogue in the realm of human affinity to the enclosure acts whereby common lands were made private. Shakespeare's play inscribes an act of spiritual enclosure, love transformed into private property. Whatever is owned may be seized. The fear of loss is integral to the principle of property and thus the threat that Iago represents comes as much from within Othello as from without; Shakespeare externalizes the already implicit fear in the figure of Iago, making the villain, in Burke's phrase, into a voice at Othello's ear. Othello and Iago, possessor and the threat of loss, are dialectically related parts of the one "fascination." Add Desdemona to the integral, Burke says, "and you have a tragic trinity of ownership in the profoundest sense of ownership, the property in human affections, as fetishistically localized in the object of possession."

Property implies theft: therein lies the play's premise. Opening in Venice, the city of fabled commercial wealth, *Othello* is structured as a series of thefts. The first is a variant of the stock comic action of the stolen daughter that Shakespeare uses also in his other play set in Venice when Jessica escapes from Shylock's house laden with ducats and jewels. Here, in an episode that foreshadows his later and more subtle arousing of Othello, Iago wakes Brabantio: "Awake! what ho, Brabantio! thieves, thieves! / Look to your house, your daughter, and your bags! / Thieves, thieves!" (1.1.79–81). And a moment after: "Zounds, sir, y'are robb'd! For shame, put on your gown; / Your heart is burst, you have lost half your soul" (1.1.86–87).

Let us note the fusion of spiritual and proprietary ideas: Desdemona is both half her father's soul and a possession equivalent to his money. Let us note, too, that so far as the play is concerned Desdemona might have no mother. She is represented as wholly her father's possession, and the principal question concerning her at the opening is whether the transfer from father to husband has been rightfully made, whether she has in fact been stolen from Brabantio or properly won. Again, the play fuses spiritual and proprietary themes when in the Senate scene the Duke decides the case on romantic principles. "I think this tale would win my daughter too" (1.3.171), he comments on Othello's speech, and when Desdemona acknowledges that she freely loves the Moor, Brabantio must yield.

The play's first movement is "The Abduction of Desdemona"; the second is "The Theft of Cassio's Name." Cassio supposes that he is wholly responsible for the loss of his reputation, but we know that Iago, plying his victim with wine, has robbed him. The presentation of Cassio as a decent man changed into a drunken madman foreshadows the action with Othello to come, specifically, the theme of diabolic possession: "O thou invisible spirit of wine, if thou hast no name to be known by, let us call thee devil! . . . To be now a sensible man, by and by a fool, and presently a beast! O strange! Every inordinate cup is unbless'd, and the ingredient is a devil" (2.3.281–308). To which Iago replies in language that plays upon the theme: "Come, come; good wine is a good familiar creature, if it be well us'd" (2.3.309–10).

In the transitional culture of the early modern period the concept of the soul is also affected by the hegemonic principle of property. Now a soul is something a person *has* as well as something a person *is*. We think, of course, of Marlowe's Faustus selling his soul by contract like an aristocrat turning his land into cash; and it may be, too, that the interest in cases of possession and exorcism at the end of the sixteenth century reveals the influence of proprietary modes of thought. In *Othello*, at any rate, the theme of diabolic possession is related to the play's concern with property. Here the ideas of soul, property, and honor join together in a complex dance of equivalences and ironies, as when Iago tells Brabantio that he has been robbed of half his soul or when Cassio speaks of his reputation as his immortal part.

The play's main action, which begins in the temptation scene when Iago at last turns to work directly upon Othello, depends upon this system of unstable equivalences. Speaking to Cassio, Iago has dismissed the loss of reputation as insignificant, but now he echoes Cassio when he proclaims the opposite to Othello:

> Good name in man and woman, dear my lord,
> Is the immediate jewel of their souls.
> Who steals my purse steals trash; 'tis something, nothing;
> 'Twas mine, 'tis his, and has been slave to thousands;
> But he that filches from me my good name
> Robs me of that which not enriches him,
> And makes me poor indeed.
>
> (3.3.155–61)

With the idea of theft thus implanted in his thoughts, Othello himself is soon speaking of robbery—"What sense had I in her stol'n hours of lust?" (3.3.338)—accusing Desdemona of filching her honor, which as her husband belongs ultimately to him, and thus of stealing also his own good name.

"I am your own for ever" (3.3.480). When at the end of the temptation scene Iago says that he belongs to Othello forever we understand that he means the opposite of what he speaks: Othello is now his. Othello believes that Desdemona has been stolen from him but the truth is that he has been stolen from himself. The demi-devil Iago has taken possession of his soul. Soon, like a classic case of demonic possession, Othello will be thrashing on the ground, foaming and raving in a fit. Soon, too, diabolic powers will in effect speak through Othello's mouth as the smooth and authoritative cadences of what Wilson Knight calls the "Othello music" yield to the staccato fragments and ugly images associated with Iago. In this way the unitary world of absolute self-possession that is recapitulated in "Farewell the tranquil mind" is split open and Othello becomes estranged not only from Desdemona but from himself. Like Spenser's Redcross knight, who is also launched into a world of doubleness, Othello is propelled into a nightmare of duplicity in which his love and his doubt are at war with each other. This process of self-alienation climaxes in Othello's suicide, the one half of his divided self executing justice upon the other as once he administered justice to the Turk in Aleppo. Thus the

If to preserve this vessel for my lord
From any hated foul unlawful touch,
Be not to be a strumpet, I am none.
(4.2.85–87)

Her naiveté and docility in the willow scene are partly a result of her confusion and fear, but perhaps also partly a protective facade behind which she waits, as she did during courtship, while determining the most appropriate and fruitful reaction to Othello's rage. The conversation and the song with its alternate last verses explore alternate responses to male perfidy—acceptance *"Let nobody blame him, his scorn I approve"*—or retaliation *"If I court moe women, you'll couch with moe men"* (4.3.51–56). Emilia supports retaliation—"The ills we do, their ills instruct us so" (l. 103)—though, like Bianca, she practices acceptance. Desdemona's final couplet suggests that she is groping for a third response, one that is midway between "grace" and "revenge," one that would be more active than acceptance yet more loving than retaliation:

God me such usage send,
Not to pick bad from bad, but by bad mend!
(4.3.104–05)

The lines are a reply to Emilia and a transformation of an earlier couplet of Iago's: "fairness and wit / The one's for use, the other using it" (2.1.129–30). Desdemona will put fairness and wit to *use* in a sense that includes and goes beyond the sexual one, acknowledging and using "bad" to heal it. Her earlier command to have the wedding sheets put on her bed seems one expression of this positive usage. Just before her death, as earlier in the handkerchief and brothel scenes, Desdemona strives to "mend" Othello's debased view of her, transforming the "sins" he accuses her of into "loves I bear to you"; a testimony to her pure, active, humble, fertile affections. But Othello recorrupts them: "And for that thou diest" (5.2.40–41).

The men's sense of identity and worth is dependent not only on their relations with women but on their bonds with other men who guarantee their honor and reputation. Vanity, rivalry, and dependence characterize the relations among all the men in the play. Jaques's portrait of the soldier aptly sums up traits which they share: "Full of strange oaths and bearded like the pard, / Jealous in honor, sudden and quick in quarrel, / Seeking the bubble reputation / Even in the canon's mouth" (2.7.149–52), traits which are those of coxcombs but grow murderous here. Cassio, of course, explicitly voices the men's concern with "the bubble reputation" and reveals how central their position and image are to their sense of identity: "I ha' lost my reputation! I ha' lost the immortal part, sir, of myself, and what remains is bestial" (2.3.255). This identity is highly vulnerable because the men view reputation as detachable, external; it is a matter of rank or title, something to be conferred—or removed—by other men. Hence Iago continues to care about the rank of lieutenant in spite of his continuing intimacy with Othello. Cassio equally relishes his title; "The lieutenant is to be saved before the ancient," he boasts (2.3.103). Othello must fire Cassio for appearances' sake and because Montano "is of great fame in Cyprus" (3.1.46). Othello's dependence on others' "rich opinion" (2.3.286) creates conflict in his love; "feather'd Cupid" potentially threatens "reputation" in the first act, and later he finds the scorn due the cuckold almost as difficult to bear as the loss of Desdemona.

Although they are neither "bearded like a pard" nor "full of strange oaths," the men in this play, in their vanity, desire the swaggering manliness which such characteristics conjure up. Iago successfully plays on the others' nervousness about this "manliness," driving them to acts of "malicious bravery" (1.1.100). He jovially calls them "man" while questioning their manhood or urging new proofs of it. He goads Cassio into "manly" drunkenness and good fellowship—"What, man, 'tis a night of revels, the gallants desire it" (2.3.39). He urges Othello, "Good sir, be a man" (4.1.65). He flatters Roderigo's manly pride: "if thou hast that within thee indeed, which I have greater reason to believe now than ever, I mean purpose, courage, and valour, this night show it" (4.2.213–16). His suggestive battle cries to Roderigo imply a connection that all the men assume between sexual and martial prowess: "Wear thy good rapier bare, and put it home. . . . fix most firm thy resolution" (5.1.2, 5); perhaps the gull's melodramatic attack on Cassio is "satisfying" even beyond Iago's "reasons," compensating him for his lack of sexual success. Inversely, cuckoldry is seen by Othello as invalidating his military glories; only the murder of Desdemona and his own suicide restore his pride in his "occupation."

Since the reputation and manliness which the men covet is achieved in competition with others, all the men are "jealous in honor, sudden and quick in quarrel." Iago's success derives largely from his ability to manipulate male rivalries, verifying his friendship with each man by shared contempt toward another. In this way, he feeds the men's need for self-esteem, insures their bond with him, and exacerbates their potential rivalries with each other. He enrages Brabantio by claiming that his friend has "robbed" his daughter. He gulls Roderigo by demeaning Othello and urging that they have common cause against him: "my cause is hearted, thine has no less reason, let us be communicative in our revenge against him: if thou canst cuckold him, thou doest thyself a pleasure, and me a sport" (1.3.366–69). He almost offhandedly belittles Othello to Cassio, Cassio to Montano, Othello to Lodovico. His entrapment of Othello begins by insinuating not Desdemona's unfaithfulness but Othello's cuckoldry, his loss of "good name." This cuckoldry triply threatens Othello: with the loss of Desdemona's love; with the supremacy of Cassio, his lieutenant, over him; and with the loss of his reputation and the scorn of other men.

Iago offers to compensate for these losses with his own love—to replace Othello's other bonds with their friendship. Iago's attack is set up when Othello demands that Iago prove his love by complying with his general's wishes (he has just been threatened by Desdemona's seeming to put similar pressure on him): "If thou dost love me, / Show me thy thought" (3.3.119–20). It concludes with Othello's attempt to replace his love for Desdemona with a vow of vengeance and a (coerced) bond with Iago, through which it seems he can restore his heroism and control by regaining the love and dependence he fears he has lost:

> IAGO: Witness, you ever-burning lights above,
> You elements that clip us round about,
> Witness that here Iago doth give up
> The excellency of his wit, hand, heart,
> To wrong'd Othello's service: let him command,
> And to obey him shall be in me remorse,
> What bloody work so ever.
>
> OTHELLO:
> I greet thy love;
> Not with vain thanks, but with acceptance bounteous.
>
> (3.3.470–78)

Iago's feigned love gives him power which Desdemona's genuine love cannot counteract; he destroys his superior by destroying Othello's belief in his own superiority and the bonds which confirm that superiority. Nowhere is his power and its roots in Othello's fear of inferiority to other men more ruthlessly and painfully demonstrated than when Iago engineers Othello's eavesdropping of his and Cassio's mockery of Bianca; here, Othello's wounded vanity, obsessive jealousy, and competitive concern for reputation and manliness coalesce in his terse asides with their sexual-martial double entendres:

> Do you triumph, Roman, do you triumph?
>
> So, so, so, so; laugh that wins.
>
> Ha' you scor'd me? Well.
>
> I see that nose of yours, but not that dog I shall throw't to.
> (4.1.118,122,126,140)

Iago likewise gains power by imposing on the play, through his bawdy, an image of heterosexuality which, like male bonds, is seen as competitive and violent. Sexuality here is not merely represented as an act of male assertion, as in *Much Ado,* or as painful debilitation, as in *All's Well That Ends Well,* but as a violent, bestial overpowering of the woman by the man which degrades both: "an old black ram / Is tupping your white ewe," "you'll have your daughter cover'd with a Barbary horse," "he hath boarded a land carrack"; Desdemona is in the "gross clasps of a lascivious Moor" (1.1.88–89; 110–11; 2.2.50; 1.1.126). This vision of sexuality comes to replace the tender, hallowed passion of Desdemona for Othello, her desire to participate in "the rites for which I love him" (1.3.257), as Othello imagines that Cassio "lie[s] with her, lie[s] on her" (4.1.38), "pluck[s] up kisses by the roots" (3.3.429). The inevitable culmination of this fantasy occurs when Othello clasps, covers, and stifles Desdemona—"Down, strumpet. . . . Nay and you strive" (5.2.80,82), silencing her "even in the bed she hath contaminated" (4.1.203)—and then kills himself.

Although the men's aggression destroys the women, their attempts at heroic violence against each other do not completely succeed. Othello vows to kill Cassio but never does, and Roderigo's murder attempt on Cassio fails. It takes Cassio and Iago together to kill poor Roderigo, and Othello cannot kill Iago. The cowardice, clumsiness, and insecurity that belie male pretensions to valor are manifested comically—as in the *Twelfth Night* duel or in the gulling of Parolles—in the hesitation of Lodovico and Gratiano to answer Roderigo's and Cassio's cries for help: "Two or three groans; it is a heavy night, / These may be counterfeits, let's think 't unsafe / To come into the cry without more help" (5.1.42–45). Even after Iago's entrance, they still hang back, ascertaining his identity (51) but ignoring his cry (thus allowing him to murder Roderigo), introducing themselves (67), discovering Cassio's identity (70), and finally coming to his side after Bianca, who has just entered (75). They still offer no assistance but only perfunctory sympathy and an anticlimactic explanation: "I am sorry to find you thus, I have been to seek you" (81).

Male friendship, like male courage, is in this play sadly deteriorated from the Renaissance ideal. In romance and comedy, the world of male friendship in which the work opens (see, for example, the *Arcadia, Two Gentlemen of Verona, The Merchant of Venice, Love's Labor's Lost*) is disrupted and transcended by romantic love. In the problem comedies, male friendship is already corrupted as friends exploit and betray each other. As *Othello* begins, romantic love already dominates, but friendship is reasserted in perverted form. Iago's hypocritical friendship for all of the men, which aims to gratify his own will and gain power over them, is the model for male friendship in the play. Brabantio's "love" for Othello evaporates when his friend marries his daughter. Roderigo intends to use Iago though he is worse used by him. Othello has no hesitation in cashiering Cassio and ordering his death. The men's vanity and rivalry, their preoccupation with rank and reputation, and their cowardice render them as incapable of friendship as they are of love.

The women, in contrast, are indifferent to reputation and partially free of vanity, jealousy, and competitiveness. Desdemona's willingness "to incur a general mock" is evident in her elopement and her defense of it, and in her request to go to Cyprus. Emilia braves scorn to defend her mistress, "Let heaven, and men, and devils, let 'em all, / All, all cry shame against me, yet I'll speak" (5.2.222–23). If Cassio's description of Bianca corresponds at all to fact, she too ignores reputation, comically, to pursue him—"she haunts me in every place . . . she falls thus about my neck; . . . so hangs, and lolls, and weeps upon me" (4.1.131–36)—and we see her brave the confusion of the night and the ugliness of Iago's insinuations to come to Cassio's side when he is wounded. Bianca's jealousy is also in contrast to the men's; instead of corroding within, it is quickly vented and dissipates, leaving her affection for Cassio essentially unchanged. Furthermore, she makes no effort to discover her rival, to obtain "proof," or to get revenge. Likewise Emilia, though expert at noting and analyzing jealousy, seems untouched by it herself. Even her argument for the single standard is good-natured; it contains little hatred of men and no personal animosity toward Iago.

Desdemona is neither jealous nor envious nor suspicious. She is not suspicious or possessive about Othello's job, his intimacy with Iago, or his "love" for Cassio, but supports all three. She seems entirely lacking in the sense of class, race, rank, and hierarchy that concerns the men and is shared by Emilia, who refuses to be identified with Bianca. She treats her father; the Duke, Othello, Cassio, Iago, Emilia, even the clown, with precisely the same combination of politeness, generosity, openness, and firmness. Emilia's and Desdemona's lack of competitiveness, jealousy, and class consciousness facilitates their growing intimacy, which culminates in the willow scene. The scene, sandwiched between two exchanges of Iago and Roderigo, sharply contrasts the genuine intimacy of the women with the hypocritical friendship of the men, while underlining the women's isolation and powerlessness. Emilia's concern for Desdemona is real, and her advice well meant, whereas Iago's concern for Roderigo is feigned, his advice deadly—"whether he kill Cassio, / Or Cassio him, or each do kill the other, / Every way makes my game" (5.1.12–14). Roderigo accepts Iago's "satisfying reasons," finding them sufficient to justify murder; Desdemona rejects Emilia's reasonable justification of wives' adultery without rejecting the concern that prompts her to offer it. In the willow scene sympathy stretches from Emilia and Desdemona to include Barbary and the protagonist of the song—all victims of male perfidy; in the Roderigo/Iago scenes, enmity reaches Cassio. In this play romantic love is destroyed by the semblance of male friendship, which itself soon disintegrates. Meanwhile, friendship between women is established and dominates the play's final scene. Othello chooses Iago's friendship over Desdemona's love temporarily and unwittingly; Emilia's choice of Desdemona over Iago is voluntary and final. Though the stakes here are higher, the friendship of Desdemona and Emilia is reminiscent of the generous, witty female friendship in the comedies, where women share their friends' hardships (Rosalind and Celia), vigorously defend their honor (Beatrice and Hero), support their strategems (Portia and Nerissa), and sympathize with and aid even their rivals (Julia and Sylvia, Viola and Olivia, Helen and Diana, Mariana and Isabella). But in *Othello,* without the aid of disguise, bedtricks, or mock deaths, the women cannot protect each other from male animosity.

Because of the men's vanity, competitiveness, and concern for honor and reputation, when they do act, they try to exonerate themselves, persistently placing blame for their actions outside themselves. Even Cassio, while abusing himself for his drunkenness, comes to personify that drunkenness as a "devil," something which invades him. Roderigo blames Iago for his failure to prosper: "Iago hurt [me]. Iago set [me] on" (5.2.329–30). Iago, at the last, instead of boasting about the execution of his grand design (as, for example, Satan does in *Paradise Lost*), tries to shift responsibility for it elsewhere—to Bianca, to Emilia, and finally, even after the facts are known, to Othello: "I told him what I thought, and told no more / Than what he found himself was apt and true" (5.2.177–78).

Othello's longing for passivity and his denial of responsibility are intertwined throughout the play. He both sees himself as passive and desires passivity. His narrative history before the senate, the basis for our original impression of the heroic Othello, describes, when closely examined, what he has suffered rather than what he has done; he speaks of "moving accidents by flood and field; / Of hair-breadth scapes 'i th' imminent deadly breach; / Of being taken by the insolent foe; / And sold to slavery, and my redemption hence" (1.3.135–38), and of his subsequent enslavement by Desdemona, whom he entertained with similar tales, for example, "of some distressed stroke / That my youth suffer'd" (1.3.157–58). Pity is indeed the appropriate response to his tale. His farewell to arms is, curiously, a farewell to "content," to "the tranquil mind" (3.3.354); and to the instruments of war; it is they who are seen as active and heroic, not himself. His vow of revenge, likening him to the "compulsive course" of the "Pontic sea," reveals the longing for external control and validation which underlies the heroic stance. In a parallel passage after his error is revealed, he again wants to be swept along by a current: "Blow me about in winds, roast me in sulphur, / Wash me in steep-down gulfs of liquid fire!" (5.2.280–81), to be consumed by hell-fire rather than by desire. Two of his significant actions in the play—the cashiering of Cassio and the murder of Desdemona—are, in a sense, "compulsive," achieved, as he himself notes, only when passion "Assays to lead the way" (2.3.198), and he feels out of control or seeks a false sense of being under the control of an impersonal "cause." Even at his suicide, when he *is* in control, he sees himself as "you" rather than "I," object rather than actor, as "being wrought, / Perplex'd in the extreme . . . one whose subdued eyes, . . . Drops tears as fast as the Arabian trees / Their medicinal gum" (5.2.246–51). In the anecdote that accompanies his suicide, Othello is actor and acted upon, hero and victim, and his action is again violent and enraged. But it is also premeditated—and gives him, at last, the command over himself he has not achieved throughout.

Desdemona's self-recriminations must be seen in the light of Othello's evasions. Critics have found them puzzling, excessive, intolerable, even neurotic, perhaps they are all of these. But her unwarranted self-accusations—"beshrew me much, Emilia, / I was (unhandsome warrior as I am) / Arraigning his unkindness with my soul; / But now I find I had suborn'd the witness, / And he's indited falsely" (3.4.148–52)—and her false assumption of responsibility for her death—"Nobody, I myself, farewell" (5.2.125) provide the sharpest possible contrast to the men's excuses. Her last request, "Commend me to my kind lord," not only conveys her forgiveness but is one final active effort to restore their mutual love. She is not, however, a willing victim and does not sacrifice herself to Othello, although she does not attribute guilt to him either. She defends her innocence and pleads for her life; but he murders her anyway.

Desdemona's cryptic lines after she is apparently dead give to her actual death some of the functions and the feel of Shakespearean mock deaths. Like the women who stage them, she defends her innocence—"A guiltless death I die" (5.2.123)—assumes responsibility for the death, and seeks to transform Othello into a "kind lord." When the audience finds that the woman it has thought dead remains alive, the poignant, momentary impression that this may be a mock death intensifies the horror of the scene. Desdemona's refusal to blame and hurt Othello is at the heart of her loving virtue. Hero, Helen, and Hermione likewise do not blame their detractors directly. But this virtue coalesces in dangerous ways with Othello's need to blame and hurt her.

From the beginning, Desdemona has viewed love as risk and challenge. She has violently uprooted herself from her father's protection and the conventional expectations of Venetian society, whereas Othello has put himself into "circumscription and confine" for her. She has initiated while Othello has responded. She is neither the "rose" or "chrysolite" of Petrarchan convention seen by Othello nor the saint extolled by critics. She sets the stage for her wooing by an extraordinarily active listening, which Othello naturally notices and describes; she would "with a greedy ear / Devour up my discourse" (1.3.149–50). She engenders his love by her own: "She lov'd me for the dangers I had pass'd, / And I lov'd her that she did pity them" (ll. 168–69); she proposes and elopes. She is the one who challenges her father directly, who determines to go to Cyprus. She moves after marriage to bring the lovers' idiom down to earth, using all of her "plenteous wit and invention" at their reunion and in the discussion of Cassio. All the characters in the play make mention of her energizing power. Cassio, hyperbolically, attributes to her the ability to influence recalcitrant nature:

> Tempests themselves, high seas, and howling winds,
> The gutter'd rocks, and congregated sands,
> Traitors ensteep'd, to clog the guiltless keel,
> As having sense of beauty, do omit
> Their common natures, letting go safely by
> The divine Desdemona.
>
> (2.1.68–73)

Othello is awed by her power to move man and beast—"She might lie by an emperor's side, and command him tasks. . . . O, she will sing the savageness out of a bear" (4.1.180–81, 184–85)—testifying, late in the play, to his ineradicable love for her. Iago, in soliloquy, attributes to her unlimited power over Othello—"she may make, unmake, do what she list" (2.3.337). And Desdemona herself, vowing support for Cassio, reveals her sense of her own persistance and controlling force:

> If I do vow a friendship, I'll perform it
> To the last article.
> (3.1.21–22)

But Desdemona's energy, assertiveness, and power are made possible by Othello's loving response to her, just as his subduing of himself to her, his "garner[ing] up" (4.2.58) of his heart is engendered by her love for him. Each has "thrive[d]" (1.3.25) in the apparent security of their mutual love, but their joyous subduing of themselves to each other leaves them vulnerable. With that certainty lost, with their responses to each other mistrusted, Othello is plunged into chaos and Desdemona into helplessness. In this crisis, he seeks to be "unhoused" again, and she refuses to acknowledge the loss of her new home: "Commend me to my kind lord" (5.2.126).

All of the women, in spite of their affection, good sense, and energy, fail to transform or to be reconciled with the men. The sexes, so sharply differentiated in the play, badly misunderstand each other. The men, as we have seen, persistently misconceive the women; the women fatally overestimate the men. Each sex, trapped in its own values and attitudes, misjudges the other. Iago acts on the hypothesis that women, on the one hand, share his concern with reputation and propriety ("Be wise, and get you home" [5.2.224], he orders Emilia) and, on the other, enact his salacious fantasies. Othello assumes, with Iago's prompting, that just as he is the stereotypical soldier, foreigner, older husband, so Desdemona will be the stereotypical mistress, Venetian, young bride. He responds to Iago's claim to knowledge about Desdemona—"knowing what I am, I know what she shall be"—with comic enthusiasm: "O thou art wise, 'tis certain" (4.1.73–74). Likewise the women attribute their own qualities to the men. Desdemona projects her lack of jealousy onto Othello. Emilia attributes to Iago her own capacity for empathy: "I know it grieves my husband, / As if the case were his" (3.3.3–4). Even Bianca, because she does not view herself as a whore in her relationship with Cassio, is surprised that he should treat her as one. Hence, although the women recognize the foolishness of the men's fancies, they are all too tolerant of them. Emilia steals the handkerchief for the sake of Iago's "fantasy" (3.3.303) and thus assures the success of his plot. Desdemona's salutation to Othello in act 3 is lamentably prophetic—"Be it as your fancies teach you, / What e'er you be, I am obedient" (3.3.89–90). He leaves her to be instructed in her whoredom.

The lost handkerchief becomes the emblem of the women's power and its loss. Both Othello's original description of the handkerchief and its part in the plot reveal that it is a symbol of women's loving, civilizing, sexual power. It has passed from female sibyl to female "charmer" to Othello's mother to Desdemona. Othello is merely a necessary intermediary between his mother and his wife—"She dying, gave it me, / And bid me, when my fate would have me wive, / To give it her" (3.4.61–63). Its creator, the sibyl, who "In her prophetic fury sew'd the work," and its next owner, the Egyptian charmer who "could almost read / The thoughts of people," reveal the source of its power in women's passionate intuitive knowledge. This knowledge, it seems, enables them to use and control sexuality. The middle ground that women find between lust and abstinence (as the men in the play cannot do) is suggested in the description of the process by which the handkerchief is made. The worms that did "breed" the silk, emblems of death, sexuality, and procreation, are "hallow'd." The thread they spin vitally and naturally from themselves is artificially improved, dyed in "mummy" which is "conserve[d] from maiden's hearts." The handkerchief then represents marital chastity—sexuality transformed by loving fidelity. Its function is to chasten and control men's love and desire:

> she told her, while she kept it
> 'Twould make her amiable, and subdue my father
> Entirely to her love; but if she lost it,
> Or made a gift of it, my father's eye
> Should hold her loathly, and his spirits should hunt
> After new fancies.
>
> (ll. 56–61).

It represents women's ability to moderate men's erratic (and erotic) "fancies," to "subdue" their promiscuity (assumed to be the norm under the double standard outlined by Emilia), and perhaps, by extension, their vanity, romanticism, jealousy, and rage as well. The handkerchief is the symbol of Desdemona's loving power over Othello:

> Excellent wretch, perdition catch my soul,
> But I do love, thee, and when I love thee not,
> Chaos is come again.
>
> (3.3.91–93)

The handkerchief is lost, literally and symbolically, not because of the failure of Desdemona's love, but because of Othello's loss of faith in that love. Once lost, the female power it symbolizes is degraded and constrained, and comedy gives way to tragedy.

After the handkerchief's original loss, all of the characters, men and women alike, misuse its power and misinterpret its symbolism, marking the disruption of all the love relationships in the play. The abuse begins when Othello pushes it aside, rejecting Desdemona's loving attempt to heal the pain on his forehead, and Emilia picks it up to give it to Iago, thereby making herself subservient to him and placing her loyalty to her husband above affection for Desdemona. Her silence about its whereabouts confirms her choice. Shakespeare's alteration of his source—removing Iago from an active role in the theft of the handkerchief and dramatizing its loss in these particular circumstances—emphasizes the handkerchief's symbolism and the active role played by Desdemona and Emilia in the misunderstandings that follow from its loss. In Iago's hands, its function is reversed; it is used to confirm his power over Emilia and Othello and to induce in Othello loathing for Desdemona. Iago's first mention of it incites Othello to reject love and embrace vengeance (3.3.441–86). Now the hero, under Iago's tutelage, proceeds to reinterpret the handkerchief as *his* love token—a pledge of his love and possession of Desdemona and of her sexual fidelity—"She is protectress of her honour too, / May she give that?" (4.1.14–15). Hence its loss provides "proof" of his suspicions. The reinterpretation continues in his altered description of its history in the last act. As he uses it to support his "cause" against Desdemona, it becomes "the recognizance and pledge of love / Which *I* first gave her . . . an antique token / *My father* gave my mother" (5.2.215–18; italics mine). It is now a symbol of the male control and love which Desdemona has betrayed; hence she must be punished—"Yet she must die, else she'll betray more men" (5.2.6).

Desdemona, too, alters her view of the handkerchief. Instinctively using it to cure Othello's pain, she almost succeeds. She "loves" the handkerchief (3.3.297) and recognizes the danger of its loss. But when pressed by Othello, she rejects its significance—"Then would to God that I had never seen it!" (3.4.75). Her rejection reflects the failure of her power. In Desdemona's earlier discussion of Cassio she was in control; now her persistence is foolish and provokes Othello's rage. Even in the early part of this scene, Desdemona deftly parries and "mends" Othello's ugly insinuations, turning his implied sexual vices into passionate virtues:

> OTHELLO: This hand is moist, my lady.
> DESDEMONA: It yet has felt no age, nor known no sorrow.
>
> . . . . . . . . . . . . . . . .
>
> OTHELLO: For here's a young and sweating devil here,
> That commonly rebels: 'tis a good hand,
> A frank one.
> DESDEMONA: You may indeed say so,
> For 'twas that hand that gave away my heart.
> (3.4.32–41)

But after the tale of the handkerchief she loses the initiative. She tries to regain it by—just barely—lying, and by changing the subject. But the attempt to calm and heal Othello fails. Her lie, like Ophelia's similarly well-intentioned lie to Hamlet, is generated by her love but signals the loss of her maiden's power and innocence; it confirms—Othello believes—his notions about female depravity, as Ophelia's lie confirms Hamlet's similar views. Both women, rejected by their lovers, do not regain the initiative in the relationship.

The handkerchief next creates conflict in the Iago/Emilia and Cassio/Bianca relationships. Both men use it, as Othello has done, to consolidate their power over women. When Emilia regrets its theft, Iago snatches it from her and dismisses her, "Be not you known on 't" (3.3.324). Cassio similarly gives orders to Bianca regarding it and dismisses her (3.4.188–89). She, though jealous, agrees to copy the work; her willingness to be "circumstanc'd" (l. 200) is a flaw which all the women share. Later, however, she returns the handkerchief in a scene parallel and in contrast to that when the handkerchief was lost. Bianca, like Othello, is jealous. She flings down the handkerchief as he pushed it aside, and it lies on the stage ignored by the couple, who go off to a possible reconciliation. But Bianca's refusal to be used by the handkerchief or by Cassio leads to a truce and a supper engagement, whereas Othello's refusal to be healed by it opens the breach in his relationship with Desdemona that culminates in her murder.

Eventually the handkerchief's original function is reestablished; it becomes the vehicle through which civilizing control is returned to the women. The reference to it by Othello in the last scene enlightens Emilia;

it ends Iago's domination of her, engenders her accusations of Othello and Iago, and enables her to prove Desdemona's faithful "amiable" love. Othello is once again "subdue[d]" to this love. Emilia, stealing the handkerchief, is catalyst for the play's crisis; revealing its theft, she is catalyst for the play's denouement.

Her reiteration of "husband" and "mistress" in the last scene emphasizes the play's central division and the "divided duty" of Emilia. When Iago's villainy is made known, she shifts her allegiance unhesitatingly. Instead of tolerating both Iago's "fancy" and Desdemona's virtue, she denounces the one and affirms the other. She questions Iago's manliness: "Disprove this villain, if thou be'st a man: / He said thou told'st him that his wife was false, / I know thou didst not, thou art not such a villain" (5.2.173–75). Then she rejects the wifely virtues of silence, obedience, and prudence that are demanded of her, "unhousing" herself:

> I will not charm my tongue, I am bound to speak:
> . . . . . . . . . . . . . . .
>
> 'Tis proper I obey him, but not now:
> Perchance, Iago, I will ne'er go home.
> (ll. 185,197–98)

Her epithet just before she is stabbed appropriately refers to all the men in the play: Iago, to whose taunts it is a response; Othello, who responds to it; and Cassio, Roderigo, and Brabantio as well:

> O murderous coxcomb! what should such a fool
> Do with so good a woman?
> (ll. 234–35)

Emilia, another "good woman," dies without self-justifications or calls for revenge; instead she testifies to Desdemona's innocence and love just as her mistress had done at her own death. Her request to be laid by her mistress, her reiteration of the willow song, and her own attempts to "by bad mend" complete her identification with Desdemona.

Emilia's story has utterly destroyed Iago's bond with Othello and foiled his attempt to "make up [his] will," (1.3.393), to complete himself by compensating for his own misshapenness through the stories that allow him to shape others. He and his fantasies are repudiated by Roderigo, by Othello, and by Emilia. Her refusal of obedience destroys Iago's plot and refutes his philosophy, which requires that she act in her own self-interest. Iago's final, Othello-like attempt to deny his wife's betrayal is to call her "villainous whore" and stab her, thus validating her confession and her epitaph for him. But this act, like all of the other events of the night, "fordoes" Iago instead of "mak[ing]" him (5.1.128). He has not eradicated Othello's love for Desdemona or turned her virtue into pitch. The deaths of Roderigo, Desdemona, Emilia, and Othello destroy the power over others which is the source of his self-engendering and identity. His final silence—"Demand me nothing, what you know, you know, / From this time forth I never will speak word" (5.2.304–5)—is, for him, the equivalent of suicide. Iago's silence, his imperviousness, his unmade-upness, his refusal to suffer, all mitigate his scapegoat function throughout the last scene, emphasizing instead his role as catalyst to Othello's tragedy. It is Othello's speech, his pain, his recreation of a self to which we attend.

While the division between Iago and Emilia is absolute after he kills her, some connections between Othello and Desdemona are reestablished in the last act. Desdemona, as we have seen, continues to affirm their relationship up to the moment of her death, and Othello in the last scene does move away from the men and toward the women. Othello, like Desdemona and Emilia, dies in pain testifying to love, whereas Iago lives, silent; Othello, like the women, stays to acknowledge at least partial responsibility for his actions, while Iago flees, accepting none. But Othello cannot abandon his masculine identity by asserting a new one: "That's he that was Othello; here I am" (l. 285). Instead of applying Emilia's accusation to himself, he stabs Iago; the two men are one in their desire to place guilt elsewhere and eliminate its bearer. With Iago's exit, Othello turns his attention, characteristically, to his honor and a suicide weapon. Emilia's death, though it reenacts Desdemona's, is a mere parenthesis in his search, scarcely noticed by him. Although male bombast is virtually silenced at the end of this play, as it is in the comedies—Iago will "never more speak word" (l. 305) and the terseness and precision of Roderigo's dying epithet for Iago ("O inhuman dog") are equaled in Cassio's epitaph for the dead Othello ("For he was great of heart")—Othello's rhetoric continues unchecked. Throughout the scene, he persists in seeing himself and Desdemona as ill-fated, "unlucky," as victims of Iago who has "ensnar'd" (l. 303) him. Desdemona is still imagined as the remote, passive, perfect object of romantic love. She is "cold, cold" as her "chastity" (ll. 276–77), associated with "monumental alabaster" (l. 5), with an "entire and perfect chrysolite" (l. 146), and with a "pearl" (l. 348). In his last speeches, his own brand of Iago's "motive-hunting," he strives to reconstitute his heroic reputation. He leaves the play exactly as he had entered it, affirming his services to the state (compare 1.2.17), confessing, asking for justice and judgment (compare 1.3.122–25), telling stories about his past, and putting his "unhoused free condition" into its ultimate "confine" for love of Desdemona. His suicide both punishes himself as an Iago-like "dog" and reasserts his identity as a decisive, just commander and a passionate lover of Desdemona: "I kiss'd thee ere I kill'd thee, no way but this, / Killing myself, to die upon a kiss" (ll. 359–60). His love remains idealistic, anxious, self-justifying—consummated "no way" but in death.

Indeed, most of the characters remain where they started—or return there. Here there is not even the tentative movement beyond folly that we find in the comedy heroes. Roderigo was upbraiding Iago in the play's first lines and is still doing so in the letter that is his last communication. Cassio has again received a promotion and is again caught up in events he does not comprehend. Brabantio, had he lived, likely would have responded to Desdemona's death exactly as he did to her elopement: "This sight would make him do a desperate turn" (l. 208). Iago, like Jaques, Malvolio, and Shylock, the villains of the comedies, is opaque and static. His cryptic last words, "What you know, you know," (l. 304) reveal no more about him than did his overexplanatory soliloquies. Desdemona, just before her death, challenges Othello as she had challenged her father and defends herself with the same straightforward precision she used before the senate:

> And have you mercy too! I never did
> Offend you in my life, . . . never lov'd Cassio,
> But with such general warranty of heaven,
> As I might love: I never gave him token.
> (ll. 59–62)

Bianca comes forth to seek Cassio at her last appearance as at her first; both times she frankly declares her affection and is brusquely dismissed. Emilia's function and attitudes do change, however, though her character perhaps does not. She moves from tolerating men's fancies to exploding them and from prudent acceptance to courageous repudiation. She ceases to function as reconciler of the views of the men and the women, and the separation between them widens.

The play's ending is tragic; but it is also cankered comedy. The final speech effects a disengagement even greater than that which is usual at the end of the tragedies. Avoiding mention of the love of Othello and Desdemona and direct reference to Othello's murder and suicide, it focuses on the "state matters" (3.4.153) which the lovers themselves earlier sought refuge in and on the punishment of Iago, who does, at this point, become a scapegoat. Lodovico asks us to see the tragedy as Iago's "work," to look foward with relish to his torture, and to avert our gaze from the bed and its significance. But the restoration of military order provides little satisfaction here. The speech does not look back over the events of the play, creating a sense of completion and exhaustion as in *Romeo and Juliet* and *King Lear;* it does not look forward to a new beginning, however equivocally, as do *Hamlet* and *Macbeth*. The conflict between the men and the women has not been eliminated or resolved. The men have been unable to turn the women's virtue into pitch, but the women have been unable to mend male fantasies. The comic resolution of male with female, idealism with realism, love with sex, the individual with society is aborted. The play concludes, not with symmetrical pairings off and a movement toward marriage beds, but with one final triangle: Emilia, Desdemona, and Othello dead on wedding sheets. We are made to look with Iago, ominously a survivor, at the "tragic lodging of this bed"; *lodging* here, with its resonance from other Shakespearean uses, concludes the play on a note of arrested growth, devastated fertility. "The object poisons sight"; it signifies destruction without catharsis, release without resolution. The pain and division of the ending are unmitigated, and the clarification it offers is intolerable. "Let it be hid" is our inevitable response.

# Shakespeare and Rhetoric: "Dilation" and "Delation" in *Othello*

*Patricia Parker*

Let us begin with a textual crux. At the threshold of the great temptation scene which is often described as the hinge of the entire play, Iago begins to set Othello "on the rack" through those pauses, single words and pregnant phrases which seem to suggest something secret or withheld, a withholding which fills the Moor with the desire to hear more:

> I heard thee say even now, thou lik'st not that,
> When Cassio left my wife. What didst not like?
> And when I told thee he was of my counsel
> In my whole course of wooing, thou criedst, "Indeed!"
> And didst contract and purse thy brow together,
> As if thou then hadst shut up in thy brain
> Some horrible conceit. If thou dost love me,
> Show me thy thought.
>
> (3.3.109–16)

In the lines that follow in this scene, what Kenneth Burke has called Iago's rhetorical technique of "Say the Word" is, in the Folio version, referred to as "close dilations, working from the heart, / That passion cannot rule" (ll. 123–24) [All citations of Shakespeare refer to *The Riverside Shakespeare*, ed. G. Blakemore Evans, unless otherwise noted]. The fact of the appearance of these "close dilations" in F, and in all the authoritative texts of the play but one, might justify our pausing for a moment over this enigmatic

---

From *Shakespeare and the Question of Theory*, edited by Patricia Parker and Geoffrey H. Hartman. 

phrase, if only because of the length and puzzlement of the commentary it has occasioned.

In the course of editorial glosses from Warburton onwards, several meanings for "dilation" have been adduced. Steevens observes that "dilations anciently signified delays," as in the phrase "dilacyon of vengeance" from the *Golden Legend,* while Malone cites Minsheu's famous Dictionary of 1617 to the effect that "to delate" (a variant spelling of "to dilate") meant simply, in English Renaissance usage, "to speak at large of anything." There is, however, one eccentric voice in this tradition of commentary: that of Samuel Johnson, who reads the Folio's "close dilations" as if it were "close delations," or "occult and secret accusations." Dr Johnson's reading, though clearly fascinating to subsequent editors, is frequently rejected on the grounds that, as Arden editor M. R. Ridley puts it, "there is no evidence of the use of the word in this, its Latin, sense" in Shakespeare's day. Ridley himself, puzzling over the Folio phrase and remarking that, since "it can hardly have been due to a mere blunder," whoever put it there must have "meant something by it," finally confesses that he has "very little idea what that was" and chooses the single other possible text ("close denotements") on the grounds (like Malone) that to this more neutral phrase at least, "no reasonable objection can be made."

It may, however, be worth delving further into these enigmatic "close dilations," if only because the term "dilate" itself appears in two other highly significant contexts in *Othello,* both as "to speak at large" and as a form of dilatoriness or delay. The former sense—the rhetorical tradition of the dilation of discourse which Shakespeare had already explicitly evoked when Egeon in *The Comedy of Errors* is asked to "dilate at full" (1.1.122) the story of his life—figures prominently in the scene in which Othello appears accused of "witchcraft" before the Senate in act 1 and tells of Desdemona's similar entreaty ("That I would all my pilgrimage dilate, / Whereof by parcels she had something heard," 1.3.153–54). The latter—postponement or delay—appears when Iago, confronted with the need to slow down an impatient Roderigo in order to effect his plot, reminds him that "we work by wit, and not by witchcraft, / And wit depends on dilatory time" (2.3.372–73).

"Dilation," then, would seem to have in other important parts of the play a resonance which includes at least two of the meanings adduced by editors for the Folio's puzzling phrase. But there is even yet more reason for dwelling upon, and for the moment within, this textual crux. Though Dr Johnson's suggestion of "dilations" as "delations" or "accusations" is frequently rejected on the grounds that there is no evidence of its use in this sense in Shakespeare's time, in fact such instances abound. And the link between judicial "delation" and rhetorical amplification or "dilation"—a linking of judicial and rhetorical as old as Cicero and Quintilian—is one exploited by none other than Shakespeare himself. *Delatare* in Latin can mean "to bring before a judge, indict, accuse"; and in the variations of Renaissance English spelling, "dilate" as well as "delate" could be used both for "to amplify, or narrate" and for "to accuse," as in the (for *Othello* highly suggestive) example "dilatit of adultry" (1536) cited by the *OED*. In other words, "close dilations" would not necessarily need to be amended to "close delations," as Johnson supposed, to be capable of suggesting both meanings—amplification and accusation—in one. Indeed, at least one Renaissance text (Bishop Hall's "Away, then, ye cruel torturers of opinions, dilaters of errors, delators of your brethren") makes it clear that, even in the most serious of contexts, the two were related closely enough to be readily available for wordplay, or even pun. And in this particular instance, the very "dilaters of error" are also thereby "delators" or accusers, in a way which might be highly suggestive for that Iago who, as one critic puts it, is "virtually an archetype of the informer," or delator, in *Othello*.

The textual crux and enigmatic phrase with which we began, then, might lead us not to mere puzzlement or to the necessity—and frequent editorial practice—of choosing one meaning *over* another, a process of elimination which so often presupposes a singularity of either definitive text or authoritative meaning, but rather to the possibility of reading *Othello* itself as if a phrase such as the Folio's "close dilations" might be a kind of semantic crossroads or freighted term suggestive of all three of those resonances—amplification, accusation, delay—which are so much a part of the unfolding of this particular tragedy. For "dilation" and "delation" in all of these related senses may be shown to be crucial not just at the level of single words and phrases which have been notoriously puzzling to commentators, but also at the more general level of this play's much-debated issues—from the criticisms of its passages of seemingly gratuitous amplification, "purple" rhetoric, or mere wordy filler, to its status as the most domestic of Shakespeare's tragedies, founded, as Rymer famously complained, upon a "trifle," to the classical problem of its apparent "double time" scheme.

Let us look, for example, at the resonance of a particular word. We have already observed that "dilation" and "delation" can summon up the sense both of accusation and of the provision of a narrative in response to interrogation. But what is even more important for the crossing of judicial and rhetorical in *Othello* is the fact that both depend on the provision of what were known as "circumstances"—a tradition which still survives in what we refer to as "circumstantial evidence" as well as in the basic principles of composition—and that Shakespeare himself founded a number of scenes on precisely this overlapping, or identity. "The circumstances are these," writes John Hoskins in his influential *Direccions for Speech and Style* (1599), reciting a list which, with minor variations, was repeated in countless Renaissance rhetorical handbooks: "the persons who and to whom, the matter, the intent, the time, the place, the manner, the consequences, and many more," and in echoing Bacon's oft-repeated dictum that "a way to amplify anything is . . . to examine it according to several circumstances," notes that such amplification "is more properly called *dilation*." But this detailing of "circumstances" was also the standard form of a legal indictment, as Shakespeare shows he knows only too well in Armado's dilated or wordy accusation of Costard in *Love's Labour's Lost* ("The time When? About the sixth hour . . . the ground Which? . . . the place Where? . . . ?" [1.1.231–48]) or in Autolycus's questioning of the frightened rustics in a passage which might have come straight out of descriptions of the "circumstances" most "commonly requisite in presentments before Justices of peace": "Your affairs there? what? with whom? the condition of that farthel? the place of your dwelling? your names? your ages? of what having? breeding? and any thing that is fitting to be known—discover" (*The Winter's Tale*, 4.4.717–20).

"Circumstances" dilate, then; but they may also indict. Both have to do with a discovery, uncovering, or bringing to light—the providing of information which could also enable the laying of one—and both frequently come as a response to interrogation or questioning, to someone's hunger, or demand, for narrative, as when Cymbeline, his curiosity aroused by the partial disclosure or "fierce abridgement" he has heard, demands to hear the whole story through, with all the "circumstantial branches, which / Distinction should be rich in," in order to satisfy his own "long interrogatories" (5.5.382–92), in a recognition scene which has to do with a mystery finally brought to light. The provision of such circumstances serves not only to amplify a narrative but to prove a case before a judge, including that judge who is the jealous husband of a woman "dilatit of adultry": Iago's promise to Othello soon after the "close dilations" of the temptation scene ("If imputation and strong circumstances / Which lead directly to the door of truth / Will give you satisfaction, you might have't" [3.3.406–8]) might thus be placed beside Leontes' conviction, in the scene of Hermione's indictment, that his conjecture "lack'd sight only," since "all other circumstances / Made up to th' deed" (2.1.176–79), or beside Iachimo's urging of Posthumus to believe his wife's infidelity from the all-but-ocular proof he will provide ("my circumstances, / Being so near the truth as I will make them, / Must first induce you to believe" [*Cymbeline,* 2.4.61–63]).

Dilation, and delation, by "circumstance," however, not only links amplification and accusation in ways highly suggestive for *Othello,* but is intimately related to the other sense of "dilation" - as "delay." Minsheu gives under "circumstance" not only "a qualitie that accompanieth a thing, as time, place, person, etc." but also "circuit of words, compasses, or going about the bush," a sense which Shakespeare exploits both elsewhere and in the opening lines of the play itself, when Iago complains of the putting off of his "suit" (1.1.9) by the wordy evasion of Othello's "bumbast circumstance, / Horribly stuff'd with epithites of war" (13–14). And this fuller resonance of "circumstance"—as the means, variously, of dilation, delation and delay—pervades a number of passages in *Othello,* from the Moor's curiously inflated "purple passage" of farewell to the "Pride, pomp, and circumstance of glorious war" (3.3.354) in a speech which dilates upon these very "circumstances" ("the plumed troops," "the neighing steed," "the spirit-stirring drum") to Iago's promise to make Othello a witness to Cassio's confession ("For I will make him tell the tale anew: / Where, how, how oft, how long ago, and when / He hath, and is again to cope your wife" [4.1.84–86]), to Cassio's fear of the interposition of delay in the pressing of his own "suit" ("Or breed itself so out of circumstances" [3.3.13–18]), to Emilia's challenge to whatever "busy and insinuating rogue" has slandered Desdemona to prove his accusation ("Why should he call her whore? Who keeps her company? What place? what time? what form? what likelihood? [4.2.137–38]), to those lines at the end of act 3 which have puzzled commentators but which—given that Cassio is engaged in attending on the "general" rather than (as in a favorite Shakespearean pun) on the circumstantial or particular, as well as submitting an impatient Bianca to further evasion and delay—also appear to pull its "circumstanc'd" within this orbit of association:

BIANCA: Leave you? Wherefore?
CASSIO: I do attend here on the general,
And think it no addition, nor my wish,
To have him see me woman'd. . . .
'Tis but a little way that I can bring you,
For I attend here; but I'll see you soon.
BIANCA: 'Tis very good; I must be
circumstanc'd.

(3.4.192–201)

This same Bianca will later be summoned by Iago either to acquit herself or to stand accused ("Come, mistress, you must tell's another tale" [5.1.125]) or, in other words, to be "circumstanc'd" in another sense as well. But the "circumstancing" of Bianca here, at the end of act 3, makes her by implication an adjunct or "addition" not just to Cassio but to the "general," a function which both catches the movement of the play from great things to small, general to particular, and also, as feminist critics of the play have seen, ultimately attaches to that Desdemona who, even as she is portrayed as the general's "general" (2.3.315), becomes increasingly an "adjunct," whose minute particulars increasingly preoccupy the "general" himself.

## II

Let us proceed from this preamble, then, to a reading of the play. It has often been remarked what an extraordinary emphasis is given in *Othello* to narrative and the demand for narrative, to the relating of a story or report. But what has still to be perceived is the relation of this demand to the crossing of rhetorical, judicial and temporal within the structure of "dilation" which the play itself so insistently exploits. The demand for narrative as the demand to know, as a response to an inquiry or interrogation, frequently calls attention both to the provision of "circumstances" and to the ferreting out of something enigmatic, hid or closed—a fact which gives to the play's oft-repeated "What is the matter?" the sense, as often elsewhere in Shakespeare, of a *materia* to be both enlarged upon and disclosed. Othello's suspicion of the "close dilations" of Iago in the temptation scene comes first from the way the Ensign seems to "contract and purse" his brow, as if he had "shut up" some "monster" in his "thought," too "hideous to be shown" (3.3.106–8). And the Moor's consequent demand to hear the whole—his suspicion that "This honest creature, doubtless, / See and knows more, much more, than he unfolds" (ll.242–43)—recalls the conventionally familiar description of dilation or amplification as an "unfolding" of something at first hermetically "wrapt up" or closed. But the play itself opens with a reference to something secret and, to the curious audience at least, unknown, as well as to a "purse," whose opening Shakespeare elsewhere links directly with the dilating or disclosing of a "matter" (*The Two Gentlemen of Verona*, 1.1.130, "Open your purse, that the money and the matter may be both at once deliver'd," or *Hamlet* on the wordy dilations of Osric: "His purse is empty already: all's golden words are spent" [5.2.131]); and it ends both with Iago's refusal to open that particular orifice again ("Demand me nothing; what you know, you know: / From this time forth I never will speak word" [5.2.303–4]) and with the promise of a further report (Lodovico's "Myself will straight aboard, and to the state / This heavy act with heavy heart relate" [ll. 370–71]).

The single most striking instance of the demand for narrative in act 2, however, both explicitly evokes the rhetorical tradition of the "dilation" of discourse and places that dilation within the context of a "delation" or accusation—Othello, accused by Brabantio before the judicial setting of the Venetian senate, and offering his story when the Duke observes that the circumstances of Brabantio's accusation are too "thin." Othello's narrative is both a response to the senate's interrogations and a recall of Brabantio's own earlier desire to hear all through ("Her father lov'd me, oft invited me; / Still question'd me the story of my life . . . I ran it through, even from my boyish days / To th' very moment that he bade me tell it" [1.3.127–33]):

> It was my hint to speak—such was my process—
> And of the Cannibals that each other eat,
> The Anthropophagi, and men whose heads
> Do grow beneath their shoulders. These things to hear
> Would Desdemona seriously incline;
> But still the house affairs would draw her thence,
> Which ever as she could with haste dispatch,
> She'ld come again, and with a greedy ear
> Devour up my discourse. Which I observing,
> Took once a pliant hour, and found good means
> To draw from her a prayer of earnest heart
> That I would all my pilgrimage dilate,
> Whereof by parcels she had something heard,
> But not intentively [$F_2$, "distinctively"]
>
> (1.3.142–55)

The Second Folio's controversial "distinctively" would only strengthen the rhetorical resonance of "dilation" here, as in Cymbeline's demand to hear all the "circumstantial branches, which / Distinction should be rich in" (5.5.382–83). The lines, as has often been remarked, summon up the figure not just of a demand for narrative but of a "greedy ear" which, juxtaposed with "Cannibals," suggests a hunger which will become more ominous when Iago begins to "abuse" Othello's increasingly insatiable "ear," just as their echo of Aeneas's "travellours tale" ($F_1$, 139) to Dido summons up a memory of a hunger for narrative potentially disastrous in its consequences. Character-based criticism would typically move from the description of Desdemona's "greedy ear"—as from those passages of Othello's seemingly uncharacteristic inflated rhetoric—to suggest what it reveals about some kind of flaw within the character concerned. But the chief import of such an image, in a scene whose "dilate" is to be echoed in act 3, might be not to reveal depths in Desdemona which would enable a psychologizing of what finally happens to her, but rather to introduce early on a reminder of the more ominous effect of such narrative dilation from an important Shakespearean intertext, and to anticipate the "witching" effect of Iago's larger unfolding of what his "close dilations" have only in "parcels," or in part, revealed.

Othello's rhetorical "dilation" in this scene is rendered apparently innocent by its outcome: dilation by "circumstances" in the judicial and accusatory setting of act 1 leads to acquittal, as part of that act's oft-remarked comic structure. But the dilation which here takes place in the context of wooing, winning, and acquittal from the law becomes, after the "close dilations" of the great temptation scene, a witching of the ear by "circumstances" which prove an accusation or "delation" rather than dismissing it, and in which the accuser father becomes that instrument of "Justice" (5.2.17) who is Othello himself.

Othello's dilation of his narrative, however, also involves the interposing of a pause or delay, as Rymer's complaint against its tedious amplification suggests, or as the scene itself repeatedly emphasizes in its surrounding reminders of the "haste-post-haste" matter (1.2.37) of the war against the Turks. And it is precisely such a slowing down which not only gives to so many of the play's speeches the sensation of having lasted longer than they have, but which also emerges in the next scene in which dilation is explicitly invoked, in lines crucial to the tension between delay and dispatch within the play as a whole:

> RODERIGO: I do follow here in the chase, not like a hound that
> hunts, but one that fills up the cry. My money is almost
> spent, I have been to-night exceedingly well cudgell'd;
> and I think the issue will be, I shall have so much
> experience for my pains; and so, with no money at all
> and a little more wit, return again to Venice.
> IAGO: How poor are they that have not patience!
> What wound did ever heal but by degrees?
> Thou know'st we work by wit, and not by witchcraft,
> And wit depends on dilatory time. . . .

Nay, get thee gone. *(Exit Roderigo.)* Two things are to
be done:
My wife must move for Cassio to her mistress—
I'll set her on—
Myself a while to draw the Moor apart,
And bring him jump when he may Cassio find
Soliciting his wife. Ay, that's the way;
Dull not device by coldness and delay.
(2.3.363–88)

Iago's emphasis on "patience" and slow working by "degrees" directly echoes the advice given earlier to Brabantio by the Duke, whose dilated or wordy *sententiae* are offered as a "grise or step" (1.3.200), while Roderigo's image of a hunt—both of its goal and of simply filling up the space between—recalls that of the earlier scene in act 2 ("If this poor trash of Venice, whom I trace / For his quick hunting, stand the putting on" [2.1.303–4]), in lines where Iago also proceeds with the gradual invention of his own end or objective, step by step ("'Tis here; but yet confus'd" [311]). Iago's stagemanaging of Roderigo (a feature not in Cinthio, but in *Othello* a reflection of his manipulation of the Moor and of the larger plot as well) depends on alternately delaying and inciting him, on both promising and putting off the completion of his "suit"—a combination suggested in the juxtaposition within these single lines of an invocation of "dilatory time" and a determination not to "dull . . . device by coldness and delay." "Thou know'st we work by wit, and not by witchcraft" links this reminder of dilation as delay to that verbal dilation which Othello earlier protests is the only "witchcraft" (1.3.169) he had used. And the entire passage is a crucial transition between Othello's delaying narrative in act 1 and the "close dilations" of act 3, when it is Othello's own impatient demand for "satisfaction" which must be met, and where Iago counsels his master both to delay the completion of Cassio's suit ("hold him off awhile" [3.3.248] ) and to "keep time in all" (4.1.92).

"Dilation," then, both in the scene in act 1 where the "post-post-haste" dispatch of the business of the state (3.46) must pause while Othello tells his tale, and in Iago's reminder of "dilatory time" in act 2, has to do with some form of postponement or putting off. And this link between verbal dilation and temporal delay itself may provide a perspective on other scenes as well. At the end of the act which includes both Othello's dilation and Desdemona's plea to be allowed to "unfold" her own story (1.3.243–44), Iago argues Roderigo out of the precipitate conclusion of suicide ("I will incontinently drown myself" [1.3.305]) by reminding him that Desdemona's marriage is not necessarily an ending ("There are many events in the womb of time which will be deliver'd" [1.3.369–70]), just as Desdemona will later counter Othello's wish for end, perfection, or conclusion ("If it were now to die, / 'Twere now to be most happy" [2.1.189–90]) with a reminder of process, dilation, or "increase" ("The heavens forbid / But that our loves and comforts should increase / Even as our days do grow" [2.1.193–95]), in a part of the play which repeatedly calls attention to a consummation both imminent and postponed. Between these two points, act 2 itself opens with a scene whose delayed climax—Othello's arrival at shore in Cyprus—involves a lengthy exchange between Desdemona and Iago which critics have frequently felt to be unnecessarily wordy bombast, padding, or filler, like the scenes of "interlarding" put in by other playwrights simply to eke out the time of the play itself. The scene, however, goes out of its way to call attention both to the space of "expectancy" (l. 41) and to its own wordiness in ways which suggest that, in a play which is elsewhere so preoccupied with words, with verbal dilation, and with waiting or delay, this might be a piece not of dramatic miscalculation but of design, part of the play's larger emphasis on what Desdemona, when the consummation of her marriage is put off, calls a "heavy interim" (1.3.258). For the space of delay or waiting here will, once the tragedy proper begins, become that even heavier interim or tormenting middle state before Othello's demand for certainty and conclusion can be satisfied, a link imagistically suggested when Othello himself, having murdered Desdemona in the very bed whose "wedding sheets" (4.2.105) recall that earlier consummation, proclaims: "Here is my journey's end, here is my butt, / And very sea-mark of my utmost sail" (5.2.267–68).

The scene, in fact, even calls attention to a particular form of amplification or dilation by "circumstances" which can come only to the "door" of truth (3.3.407)—that of the *blazon:*

> MONTANO: But, good lieutenant, is your general wiv'd?
> CASSIO: Most fortunately: he hath achiev'd a maid
> That paragons description and wild fame:
> One that excels the quirks of blazoning pens,
> And in th' essential vesture of creation
> Does tire the ingener.
>
> (2.1.60–65)

The Folio's "ingeniuer" or inventor highlights both the activity and the potential insufficiency of "invention" even before Iago's own ominous figure for his *inventio* ("my invention / Comes from my pate as birdlime does from frieze" (ll. 125–26), in lines which recall his earlier invocation (1.3.369–70) of dilation or unfolding as a bringing to birth ("my Muse labors, / And thus she is deliver'd" [2.1.127–28] ). The wordy paradoxes (l. 138) which he proceeds to deliver again echo those "sentences" which in rhetoric serve to amplify, but which Brabantio observes are only "words" ("words are words; I never yet did hear / That the bruis'd heart was pierced through the ear" [1.3.216–19]). And Cassio's reminder of the insufficiency of that form of verbal amplification known as the *blazon* is followed precisely by Iago's extended rhetorical description of women in this scene of waiting or delay, a description whose climax—after a set piece amplified over several lines—is proclaimed by Desdemona herself to be a "most lame and impotent conclusion" (l.161). What is here, however, ominously termed the very "vouch" or testimony of "malice itself" (l. 146) anticipates Iago's later "dilations" in the temptation scene, a description or merely verbal report of this same Desdemona in which nothing but words alone will lead Othello into a swoon, in lines which reaffirm the insufficiency of words just at the moment of their greatest power over him, and which end in a kind of ironic *blazon* ("It is not words that shakes me thus. Pish! Noses, ears and lips . . . [he falls down]" [4.1.41–43] ).

## III

The scene of Othello's dilated narrative before the senate in act 1 unfolds, as we have said, in an ultimately comic context where the provision of "circumstances" provides the means of acquittal. But act 1 itself also provides instances of a more sinister or dubious reporting of events not present to the eye, or happening offstage, from the rousing of Brabantio through mere description to the conflicting reports of the Turkish fleet in scene 3. And even before the "close dilations" of the temptation scene, *Othello* keeps our attention not only on the provision of narrative but also on the demand for "circumstances" in response to an interrogation in the scene of the night brawl in act 2, where it is now Othello rather than Brabantio who demands repeatedly to know "What is the matter?" (2.3.164, 176, 192) and to have an "answer" (l. 196) to his interrogations ("What . . . How . . . who . . . ?" [ll. 164–70]), to ferret out the circumstances of an action he has not been able to see with his own eyes.

It is, of course, the accusation and judgment of Cassio in this scene which leads directly to those "close dilations" which as amplifications only partial, "close," or incomplete have as their immediate effect the catching of Othello's own "greedy ear," just as the story heard only in "parcels" had earlier filled Desdemona with the desire that he would "all" his narrative "dilate." So insistent is the resonance of rhetorical dilation or "unfolding" as the temptation scene proceeds—as it is, indeed, throughout the play as a whole—that we might begin to speculate on why this might be so in this Shakespearean tragedy in particular. Rhetorical dilation or *copia* is a principle of both invention and "increase," just as signs are notorious minims, capable of suggesting so much more beyond themselves. But as *Othello* frequently reminds us, jealousy is also founded on a principle of enlargement ("Trifles light as air / Are to the jealous confirmations strong / As proofs of holy writ" [3.3.322–24]). And the Ensign Iago's "dilations" open up a sense of something much larger than can be unfolded or shown, a disproportion finally figured in the "trifle" of the handkerchief (*Desdemona:* "What's the matter?" / *Othello:* "That handkerchief" [5.2.47–48]), a matter or *materia* both enlarged and itself the visual evidence of Desdemona's crime, a showing forth or exposure to the eye of something which cannot in itself be seen. Iago's "close dilations" neither completely hide nor completely reveal—like, indeed, a *jalousie*—and this sense of movement from a partial tantalizing glimpse to a fuller disclosure is part of one of the most influential descriptions of rhetorical dilation itself: that it is, as Erasmus remarks in the *De Copia*, "just like displaying some object for sale first of all through a lattice or inside a wrapping, and then unwrapping it and opening it out and displaying it more fully to the *gaze*" ("ac totam *oculis* exponat").

The plot of jealousy in *Othello*, moreover, is one which not only repeatedly invokes the language of rhetorical amplification or dilation, but also one which substitutes such unfolding for more direct seeing or "ocular proof" ("Villain, be sure thou prove my love a whore; / Be sure of it. Give me the ocular proof" [3.3.359–60]). And the sense of dilation by "circumstances" as a transforming of the ear into a substitute *oculus* or eye, of providing that form of vivid description which in Latin is *evidentia* but which Puttenham translates more ominously into English as "Counterfeit Representation," runs through the entire rhetorical tradition. It is significant, then, that when Othello makes his demand for "satisfaction"—"Make me to see't; or (at the least) so prove it / That the probation bear no hinge, nor loop, / To hang a doubt on" (3.3.364–66)—Iago graphically represents to him the impossibility of a more direct gazing ("Would you, the supervisor, grossly gape on? / Behold her topp'd?" [395–96]), just as he had roused Brabantio with nothing more substantial than that vivid description of "an old black ram" tupping his "white ewe" (1.1.88–89), and offers instead precisely that form of "evidence" which is *evidentia*, those "strong circumstances / Which lead directly to the door of truth" (3.3.406–7). Dilation as an unfolding or showing forth of what was secret, closed or hid involves in so many of its charged descriptions an almost prurient sense of discovery, disclosure, or exposing to the eye. Erasmus's "unwrapping it and opening it out and displaying it more fully to the gaze" is joined by Peacham's description of dilation as "an apt and ready forme of speech to open the bosome of nature and to shew her branches, to that end they may be viewed and looked upon, discerned and knowen." And both are only too suggestive beside the language of *Othello* as it moves forward from the insinuations of Iago in this scene—a showing forth of the private or "behind doors" suggested in the *double entendres* which surround the handkerchief itself, that "thing" which Emilia offers to her husband (3.3.301–2).

Such "ocular demonstration" or vivid description also, however, elides the distinction between false report and true, since it is capable of depicting fictional—or purely invented—events as if they were actually present before the eye. It is crucial to remember that such dilation by description, or counterfeit representation, is for this reason the master trope and illusion of drama itself, just as it is—as so often in *Othello* as it proceeds—the rhetorical instrument of messengers in tragedy, of the bearers of reports of what cannot be directly seen or shown. Iago is not only the "delator" or accuser of Desdemona but, as has been so often remarked, the dramatist within the play itself, not just in his manipulation of haste and "dilatory time," but also in his provision of such vivid details and reports—to Brabantio, to Roderigo, and ultimately to Othello himself. And this dilation by circumstances will be as well the delation of Desdemona which will enable Iago, like that mysterious "Signior Angelo"—the messenger of another offstage event in act 1—to put his hearer in "false *gaze*" (1.3.19).

This link between that aspect of dilation which is the provision of vivid details and the ability—like jealousy itself—to create "much" out of "little" *(ex paucis sententiis plures factae, ex paucis membris numerosiora)* might lead us, finally, to suggest a relation between this play's insistent reminders of rhetorical dilation and the famous problem of its apparent "double time" scheme, the fact that there is simply no time for Desdemona to have had the "stol'n hours of lust" of which Othello suspects her (3.3.338), or to be guilty of his accusation that "she with Cassio hath the act of shame / A thousand times committed" (5.2.211–12). *Othello* observes the dramatic unities of time and place to an extent unusual in Shakespeare, and part of the sheer space given to narrative "unfolding" or report results from the fact that, in this contracted space, so much less can be directly seen on stage and must therefore be represented in words. Rymer complained of the tedious length of Othello's own narrative dilation—his vivid description of offstage and hence unseen events—in act 1. But it may be that, far from committing the lapse of which Rymer accuses him, Shakespeare may instead very early on in *Othello* be calling attention to the difference between narrative time, or dilation, and the more compressed dramatic time in which there may not be time, or space, for the whole story to be revealed.

Cymbeline's desire to hear all of a story's "circumstantial branches," like Desdemona's hunger to hear Othello "dilate" all of a narrative she has heard only in part, comes as a result of the tantalizing "fierce abridgement" he has heard, and his frustration is that the "time" and "place" will not be large enough for such enlargement. In its dramatic context, this sounds very much like the problem of abridgement, of contracted time and place, which is the mode of drama itself—a space in which the "circumstances" or multiple details can only be suggested. The rhetorical handbooks repeatedly speak of dilation or amplification by circumstances as a means of suggesting a multitude of details behind or within a single brief sentence or phrase—as when a contracted general statement (such as "the city was taken by storm") is "opened up" to reveal that crowd of vivid details ("flames pouring through houses and temples, the crash of falling buildings") which so effectively move the passions of a judge. In *Othello,* where Iago's "close dilations" function to suggest that so much more lies behind what has been seen or shown, the effect of that disproportion which we call "double time" might be not just the combination in the play of a sense of haste and a contrasting sense of waiting or delay, but also the creation of that rhetorical technique which, like jealousy itself, is capable of suggesting precisely such multiplicity. Francis Bacon, ever conscious of the potentially specious and even dangerous effect of such "dilation," notes the darker side of its ability to generate much out of little: "It often carries the minde away, yea, it deceyveth the sence," leaving "a suspition, as if more might be sayde then is expressed," a description of the power of "circumstances" to "deceive" which might well be set beside the inferences and insinuations of Iago in this play. *Othello* may be not only the most domestic, or "trifling," of all of Shakespeare's tragedies, but the single most powerful Renaissance instance of the tragic potential of this technique.

## IV

The effect of Iago's only partial or "close dilations" is to put Othello in that tormenting middle state or "heavy interim" of uncertainty and doubt ("I swear 'tis better to be much abus'd / Than but to know't a little" [3.3.336–37])—a state of partial knowledge or half-glimpses which leads to his demand for certainty and proof ("I'll have some proof . . . / I'll not endure it. Would I were satisfied!" [3.3.385–90]). As the temptation scene progresses, what is there termed a "foregone conclusion" (l.428) increasingly takes the form of a jumping to conclusion, of a proleptic or already accomplished closure in which the loss of Desdemona herself slips from future to past tense ("She's gone. I am abus'd, and my relief / Must be to loathe her" [3.3.267–68]; "Now do I see 'tis true. Look here, Iago, / All my fond love thus do I blow to heaven . . . / 'Tis gone" [ll. 444–46] ); in which the imagery is increasingly of an impatient and even compulsive rushing to end or conclusion ("Like to the Pontic Sea" [ll.453–60]), or of those extremes of black and white, heaven and hell, which ironically echo Brabantio's earlier demand to be "satisfied"; and in which the sense of a closed system, or collapse of the space between a question and its answer, is echoed by the seemingly gratuitous scene of wordplay which immediately follows this scene (DESDEMONA: "Can you inquire him out, and be edified by report?" CLOWN: "I will catechize the world for him, that is, make questions, and *by them* answer" [3.4.14–16].

A virtual replaying-in-little of the demand for narrative, in answer to an accusation or "delation," and as a means of ferreting out the truth, is provided in the course of the play's final acts—both in Emilia's demand for the "circumstances" that would prove Desdemona's guilt (4.2.137–38) and in Iago's promise to Othello that he shall overhear Cassio's confession in detail ("Where, how, how oft, how long ago, and when / He hath, and is again to cope your wife" [4.1.84–86] ), in a scene which repeatedly calls attention to the unfolding of a tale ("I will make him tell the tale anew. . . . Now he importunes him / To tell it o'er . . . now he begins the story"). Desdemona's desire to have Othello dilate his narrative was fanned by her hearing only "parcels" of a conversation she could not hear, at first, in full; but in contrast to Desdemona, what Othello gets is only those partial or "close dilations" on which he constructs the whole assumption of her guilt, rather than that fuller disclosure which, as the scene of her death reminds us, Cassio is never summoned to provide ("his mouth is stopp'd" [5.2.71]). In the temptation scene itself, when Iago says that, though he cannot provide direct or "ocular proof," if "imputation and strong circumstances / Which lead directly to the door of truth / Will give you satisfaction, you might ha't" (3.3.406–8), more than one reader has surmised that Othello in this image is led in imagination to stand outside the closed bedroom door. After the scene of Cassio's supposed confession, and hence of the demanded proof ("be sure thou prove my love a whore" [3.3.359]), Othello goes beyond the "door" to which "circumstances" alone could lead him, in that scene in Desdemona's chamber in which she has indeed changed places with the Bianca of which Cassio had earlier spoken, and in which Othello now treats her as that "subtile whore" (4.2.21) who keeps her "chamber" secret.

There is, finally, as the tragedy moves towards its ending, an increasing sense of the need to keep "dilation" itself under control, both to prevent further amplification or unfolding and to bring an end to delay. Othello's demand for "proof" and "satisfaction" not only foreshortens time in its rush to conclusion (his "Within these three days let me hear thee say / That Cassio's not alive," answered by Iago's "My friend *is dead;* 'tis *done* at your request" [3.3.472–74]); but in the scenes leading up to Desdemona's death, the terrible sense of being "on the rack" of uncertainty or doubt is joined by a determination not to allow time for further discourse ("Get me some poison, Iago, this night. I'll not expostulate with her, lest her body and beauty unprovide my mind again" [4.1.204–6]). The final scenes multiply the sense of both a waiting or delay and of impatience with it—from Cassio's desire "not [to] be delay'd" in the satisfaction of his "suit" (3.4.110–14) and Desdemona's counsel of "patience" immediately following the temptation scene, to Bianca's complaint of the "tedious" waiting upon Cassio in the scene in which she "must be circumstanc'd" (3.4.201), to Roderigo's frustration with Iago's continuing delay ("thou doffest me with some device" [4.2.175]) and his final determination to "no longer endure it" (l. 178).

Iago's plot, then, depends not only on "dilatory time" and on those "close dilations" which lead Othello to suspect that he knows more than he "unfolds," but finally also on keeping dilation—in both senses—under strict control, on moving quickly enough both to prevent Roderigo from making himself "known" directly to Desdemona (4.2.197) and to forestall any further "unfolding" ("the Moor / May unfold me to him" [5.1.21]). This sense of the need to limit "dilation" as the play moves towards its tragic ending includes the invocation of the misogynist topos of stopping the mouths of women and their proverbial *copia verborum*—a topos significantly evoked much earlier, in that scene of verbal dilation and delay on shore at Cyprus (2.1.100–112), and kept in mind through Desdemona's pledge to Cassio to "talk" her husband "out of patience" in his cause

(3.3.22–26): it extends, as *Othello* moves towards that end, from the call to keep Bianca from "railing" in the street, to Iago's command to Emilia to "speak within door" and "charm" her "tongue," to the violent and literal stopping of the mouth of Desdemona in her death. It also involves the invocation of yet another form of controlling the extent of dilation, a recapitulation of the sense of strict linear movement from beginning to end, cause to consequence, which pervades the language of the play as a whole, from the punning "sentences" of act 1 which are a form not just of verbal amplification but also of "doom," a syntax of movement toward what the play will term its own "bloody period" (5.2.358); to Iago's repeated manipulation of the model of sequence or succession, of movement from a premise or "position" to a conclusion; to the simultaneously logical, discursive and judicial resonance of the "cause" ("It is the cause, it is the cause, my soul" [5.2.1]) from which Othello finally proceeds to that "period." Dilation in the handbooks is a principle of fertility, *copia,* and increase: but the prescriptions for it—including the forms of its marshalling in the service of a cause, accusation or proof—repeatedly caution toward its ordering or disposition as at least in part a means of keeping that potential fertility, or expansion, within bounds. And the controlled linearity of the movement from cause to consequence, beginning to end, is part of the tragic momentum of *Othello*'s own culminating scenes, a momentum which distinguishes it, as tragedy, from a romance like *The Winter's Tale,* which shares with it the motif of jealousy and its jumping to conclusions, but then provides a dilated interval or second chance, an extension or enlargement which ultimately averts that tragic consequence.

Iago's plot as a whole, then, involves what we might call—in that term suggested by the Folio's controversial text—a technique of "close dilations," an unfolding just far enough to suggest much more than can be shown, and then, in the final acts, a countermovement to dilation, the prevention both of further discourse and of delay. The tragedy's final scene both brings the movement from cause to consequence to its final tragic end and provides to Othello's ear, only when it is too late, the details of a larger unfolding, as Roderigo's "letters" are found and Emilia refuses, finally, to "hold [her] peace" (ll. 218–22). The only respite or delay of doom and "justice" offered to Desdemona in this scene is for the purpose of confession (5.2.54–57), a confession in which Othello himself assumes the role of that power whose judgment is traditionally put off for such a purpose. And the play's ending virtually heaps up its instances of discourse withheld or demanded and discourse as only temporarily putting off—in Iago's definitive refusal to speak (5.2.303–4), in the reiteration of the judicial power of the state to force that narrative from him ("Torments will ope your lips" [l. 305]), and finally in that speech in which Othello himself, as in the dilation of his story in act 1, momentarily enacts a pause ("Soft you; a word or two" [l. 338]) before the "bloody period" (l. 358) of his suicide.

The controlling or repressing of dilation as the play moves to its own ending has what might almost be seen as its logical conclusion in Iago's "Demand me nothing; what you know, you know" (l. 303)—a withholding of further discourse which has caught the hungry ear of critics determined to ferret out the secret of the Ensign's apparently motiveless malignity; while the play's concluding line—its promise of still more relation or report—places the emphasis yet once again on the telling, or repetition, of a tale, to listeners not present at the events themselves. "Dilation" and its controlling is, much more centrally than has been recognized, a feature of that self-reflexiveness which Calderwood has called Shakespearean "metadrama," not just a strategy of the plays themselves but a partial index to those differences we call distinctions of "genre." In comedy—such as *The Comedy of Errors,* which Othello's narrative dilation in this play's comic opening act recalls—it is frequently a principle of respite and reprieve from law and judgment, however marshaled towards closure in a final recognition scene. In *Othello,* the coincidence of dilation with delation—of amplification with accusation—comes something closer to what Derrida calls the demand for narrative as the power of the police, that form of disclosure or bringing to light which Shakespeare elsewhere links with comic representatives of the law, but which here becomes something much more powerful, and sinister, in its effect.

Approaching the language of Shakespeare's plays is often a matter of exercising the critic's own native wit or word-wariness, often inspired guess. More historical investigations of its immersion in the language of rhetoric have all too often, at least until recently (and in work inspired in part by the return to rhetoric in modern theory), been restricted to refuting the charge of Shakespeare's small Latin and less Greek, or simply to listing a multitude of tropes and devices, without exploring the larger implications of their presence within specific plays. Rhetoric in the Renaissance is inextricably embedded in other discourses—of logic and politics, of theology and the ideology of sexual difference: when it speaks not only of dilation, or of fertile *copia,* but of *ordo* and "distribution," it needs to be heard on all of these levels, for it is a language which Shakespeare knew intimately enough both to manipulate and, frequently, to undermine. For the critic, familiarity with it, and investigations such as the present one, are only the beginning.

# Othello

## *Anthony Hecht*

Othello . . . is an odd amalgam of not easily reconcilable traits, and this may be said to be one of the most conspicuous things about him. While everywhere it is noted that he is given to self-dramatization, Iago, who has no affection for him, admits that he "is of a free and open nature / That thinks men honest that but seem to be so." Which is to say, he is both guileless and guileful. There is no question of his courage, nor of his weakness. Some of the contradictions about him will evince themselves in the very style of his speech, but in general I think they may be divided under two headings: the Christianized Moor and the "Roman" General.

### The Christianized Moor

It seems to me evident that an Elizabethan audience would not have been willing to grant Othello the unlimited admiration he receives from Cassio, Desdemona, the Duke, and his senate at the beginning of the play. He would have been recognized from the start as an anomaly, not only "an extravagant and wheeling stranger / Of here and everywhere," who has no real home, and therefore no civic allegiance, but, far more suspiciously, one who, had things only been slightly different (and perhaps more normal) would have been fighting on the enemy side, with the Turks and against the Venetians. Not only are we invited to share this edgy feeling, we are led to believe that Othello himself is not quite at ease in any society except that of military action, and his uneasiness is expressed, now and again, in a baroque and unnecessarily contorted syntax and diction. His manner of speech is remarked on within the first fifteen

---

From *Obbligati: Essays in Criticism*. © 1986 by Anthony E. Hecht. Atheneum, 1986.

lines of the play by Iago, who speaks contemptuously of his "bombast circumstance / Horribly stuff'd with epithets of war." But it is not only to military matters that this eccentricity applies. Othello's first speech in the play (aside from a brief half-line) is an example of the sort of knotted constructions that stand out as ungainly and unnatural. In response to Iago's warning that Brabantio is rousing sentiments against Othello's marriage, Othello declares,

> Let him do his spite.
> My services, which I have done the signiory,
> Shall out-tongue his complaints; 'tis yet to know—
> Which, when I know that boasting is an honour,
> I shall promulgate—I fetch my life and being
> From men of royal siege, and my demerits
> May speak unbonneted to as proud a fortune
> As this that I have reach'd; for know, Iago,
> But that I love the gentle Desdemona,
> I would not my unhoused free condition
> Put into circumscription and confine
> For the sea's worth.

I submit that this is far from straightforward speech, and in it is couched no mere self-respect, nor even boasting under the guise of refusing to boast, but what I think was meant to be immediately recognized as a ludicrous and nervous vanity. We get no more about Othello's genealogy, nor any glimpse of his family life, since by his own admission he was given over to the profession of war from the age of seven. But to claim that the cream of Moorish society was the equal of the best of Venetian nobility would probably have provoked the sort of smile based on racial and national snobbery that has a central place in this play. "Unbonneted" occurs nowhere else in the entire Shakespeare corpus, and would normally mean taking the bonnet *off* as a sign of obeisance before a superior. In the present context, as has been noted, it must mean *without* taking the bonnet off, since Othello is insisting that he need defer to no one. Either he is using an exoticism with which we are unfamiliar, or he is misusing the language. There is, in any case, a manifest self-consciousness about his speech, with its intricate pattern of "'tis yet to know, . . . which, when I know . . . for know, Iago," that marks it off from the speech of all others in the play—except Iago's when, out of malicious pleasure and spite, he parodies Othello to his face in speeches Othello is too preoccupied to recognize as parody, but which we are free to notice. I shall take note of these in due course. We have the unassailable fact of Othello's Moorishness, a fact conventionally assimilated to negroid features, and undisguisedly identified with black skin ("an old black ram / Is tupping your white ewe") and about which, since it cannot be concealed, Othello appears to be defensively proud.

But Othello is not simply a Moor; he is a Christian, and the play abounds with imagery of Christian salvation and damnation, and in the almost continuous confrontation of heaven and hell. When Othello offers to tell the story of his courtship, and reveal what magic charms he has used to win Desdemona (a taunt he is delighted to prove baseless and show that he is more sophisticated than to dabble in such primitive rites) he sends Iago to bring Desdemona to testify for herself, and says,

> And till she come, as truly as to heaven
> I do confess the vices of my blood,
> So justly to your grave ears I'll present
> How I did thrive in this fair lady's love,
> And she in mine.

It had best be said immediately that the quarto substitutes "faithful" for "truly," and omits the entire line, "I do confess the vices of my blood." But that line is by no means the only index of Othello's Christian orientation. Addressing the Duke and senators he swears, "Vouch with me, heaven," and says to them, "heaven defend your good souls." Agreeing to Desdemona's prayer that their marital happiness may continue and grow, he declares, "Amen to that, sweet powers!" More explicitly still, when called from his marriage bed by the brawl of Cassio and Roderigo, he calls everyone to order in the following terms:

> Why, how now, ho! From whence ariseth this?
> Are we turned Turks, and to ourselves do that
> Which heaven hath forbid the Ottomites?
> For Christian shame put by this barbarous brawl!

There would, I venture to suppose, be something slightly galling to an Elizabethan audience in having a Moor lecture his gentile associates and subordinates on Christian behavior. If "turn Turk" means "turn renegade," one wonders what this might have meant, coming from the mouth of a Moor, since the Moor himself must have turned renegade to become a Christian. He is, in all probability, a Morisco, or New Christian, a breed regarded without much trust by the Christian community at that time. In this regard I should like to cite some passages from Henry Kamen's account of the Spanish Inquisition. In his chapter on the Moors he says,

> Charles V finally on 13 September 1525 issued orders that Moors were no longer to be tolerated in Spain except as slaves, and measures for their conversion were to be set on foot. This was followed on 25 November by a decree for the expulsion of all Moors from Valencia by 31 December, and from Catalonia and Aragon by 31 January 1526. The unfortunate Moors came forward in their thousands to accept a religion which they neither believed nor loved nor intended to practice. . . .
>
> In Valencia many Moriscos spoke only Arabic and knew no "christianesch"; but even those who spoke Valencian considered Arabic their mother tongue. In addition to the widespread ignorance of Christianity, therefore, there existed a language problem. The Spanish priests spoke no Arabic and most of them were like the bishop of Orileula, who considered it the duty of the Moriscos, as subjects of the Spanish crown, to learn the Spanish tongue. In their communities the Moriscos still retained all the practices of their old faith as well as the traditional social customs which set them apart from the Christian population. This distinctive existence made it impossible to assimilate them into the body of a religiously united Spain.

Professor Kamen goes on to list the impossible burdens placed not only upon Moors but even upon New Christian Moriscos both by the Spanish crown and by the Inquisition, and then he declares,

> Faced with Christianity of such a merciless nature they resorted inevitably to rebellion and flight. In the Cortes [or local parliament] at Monzón in 1542 it was stated categorically that Moriscos had been fleeing abroad to join the Turks, "because of the fear they have of the Inquisition." They returned to their friends abroad, to the Muslim kingdoms in north Africa and the near East, and to the Barbary pirates.

The Moors and the Turks were united in religion, and the traditional enemies of Christian Europe, having pressed as far as Tours from the south, and as near as Vienna from the east. It was against their heresy and their possession of the Holy Land that the Crusades were directed, and the Crusades are remembered in this play by the word "crusadoes," the name of a coin, uttered by Desdemona, and recalling inevitably the Christian campaign against infidels.

The treatment of the Moors as well as of the New Christian Moriscos in Spain was very much like the treatment of Jews and those converts among the Jews who became New Christians, *marranos* or *conversos*. The parallel has its relevance. Kamen writes,

> The converso was not simply a convert. Christian society was all too conscious that the converted Jews had in reality been forced unwillingly into their new faith: the converso was, from the first, therefore, regarded with suspicion as a false Christian and a secret judaizer or practicer of Jewish rites. The conversos or New Christians soon came to be distrusted even more than the Jews, for they were considered to be a fifth column within the body of the Church. New words were coined to describe them, the most common being *marranos,* a word which probably derives either from the Hebrew *maranatha* (the Lord comes) or from a description of the Jews as those who "marran" or mar, the true faith. The conversos were thus resented by the body of Old Christians, who distrusted the sincerity of their faith and objected to the prominent part they played in Christian society. Although no longer Jews in religion, they now began to be subjected to all the rigors of antisemitism.

Moors and Jews were, accordingly, in a logically hopeless position, and regarded as infidels whether they converted or not, because, in the words of Samuel Butler in *Hudibras,*

> He that complies against his will
> Is of his own opinion still.

Brents Stirling, in an introduction to *The Merchant of Venice* in the Penguin edition, writes,

> London playgoers of 1596–97 would have included many who jibed at Dr. Roderigo Lopez, the Christianized Portuguese Jew and royal physician, who in 1594 was convicted on doubtful evidence of plotting to poison Queen Elizabeth. As Camden tells the story, just before Lopez was publicly hanged and quartered at Tyburn he protested from the scaffold that "he had loved the Queen as he loved Jesus Christ," an appeal, Camden

> adds, "which from a man of Jewish profession was heard not without laughter."

The same Elizabethan audience that could laugh at Lopez would regard Othello's ostentatious Christianity as suspect, unctuous, and offensive. They might even expect that sooner or later this show of piety would break down under pressure because it was not "natural" or "normal" in a Moor. What we know of Othello's background is sketchy, but it involves "being taken by the insolent foe; / And sold to slavery. . . ." That foe is not identified, but it is likely to be the Christian opponent; and if Othello is now himself a Christian, he is likely to have become so under the duress of slavery, as was the case with many others. If there were those who felt that Othello was not truly entitled to his Christian posture, they would have heard the following speeches with mounting irritation and derision.

> This hand of yours requires
> A sequester from liberty, fasting and prayer,
> Much castigation, exercise devout;
> For here's a young and sweating devil here,
> That commonly rebels.

> Naked in bed, Iago, and not mean harm?
> It is hypocrisy against the devil:
> They that mean virtuously, and yet do so,
> The devil their virtue tempts, and they tempt heaven.

(The last line here recalls the temptation of Christ in the wilderness.)

> Come, swear it, damn thyself;
> Lest, being like one of heaven, the devils themselves
> Should fear to seize thee. Therefore be double-damned—
> Swear thou art honest.

> Had it pleased heaven
> To try me with affliction, had they rain'd
> All kinds of sores and shames on my bare head,
> Steep'd me in poverty to the very lips,
> Given to captivity me and my utmost hopes,
> I should have found in some place of my soul
> A drop of patience.

> You, mistress,
> That have the office opposite to Saint Peter,
> And keep the gates in Hell.

OTHELLO: Have you pray'd tonight, Desdemon?
DESDEMONA: Ay, my lord.
OTHELLO: If you bethink yourself of any crime
Unreconciled as yet to heaven and grace,
Solicit for it straight.
DESDEMONA: Alack, my lord, what may you mean by that?
OTHELLO: Well, do it, and be brief; I will walk by.
I would not kill thy unprepared spirit.
No, heaven forfend! I would not kill thy soul.

This is merely a representative selection of quotations, but enough, I think, to suggest that if an audience looks for, and hopes to find, any crack in Othello's moral armor—if that audience expects to congratulate itself on its Iago-like, cynical good sense in doubting the stamina and authenticity of this Christian stance—its meanest and crudest hopes will be more than realized.

In spite of his early irony in regard to Brabantio's accusation that he, Othello, would employ "magic" to win Desdemona, with all the lofty suggestions that he is above such primitive traffic and belief (though Brabantio appears to believe it enough to offer it as a charge), he nevertheless tells Desdemona, in regard to the handkerchief he gave her, that "There's magic in the web of it." It is irrelevant whether Othello himself believes this or not; he wants Desdemona to think he believes it, and so he is acting as if he thought it were true, and wished others to believe he thinks it true. It is a signal reversion to something explicitly un-Christian, and its disconnection with Christianity is made as clear as possible:

A sibyl that had number'd in the world
The sun to course two hundred compasses,
In her prophetic fury sewed the work;
The worms were hallowed that did breed the silk;
And it was dyed in mummy which the skilful
Conserved of maiden's hearts.

Within a short time he has turned overtly savage: "I'll tear her all to pieces!" and "I will chop her into messes!" And, finally, by way of clinching the matter, after having told Desdemona that he will not kill her soul, and that she will be allowed what the basest prisoner is allowed, the right to make her peace with God before execution, he ignores his promise, breaks his word, and murders her before she has had a chance to pray. In these telling speeches and acts he has behaved as if his Christianity were never deeply believed, and therefore all the more dishonorable and affected in retrospect.

## THE "ROMAN" GENERAL

By this epithet I mean to suggest several things about Othello. There is the high premium he puts on "honour," in the Roman military tradition, and his deeply professional feeling about soldiery. In this he bears a resemblance to other Shakespearean figures in the Roman and History plays; and his concern with "honour" is one that preoccupies Shakespeare over a large part of his career. In this connection Othello makes use of classical imagery, and it is used about him by others. But most strikingly of all, he gives way to, or affects, a sort of rhetoric, a distortion or inflation of speech that particularly irritates Iago, and which we cannot fail to take notice of.

After the arrival in Cyprus of the main segment of the Venetian fleet, and of all the main characters but Othello himself, Cassio makes an exhilarated and grateful prayer of welcome and protection for Othello and Desdemona:

> Great Jove, Othello guard,
> And swell his sail with thine own pow'rful breath,
> That he may bless this bay with his tall ship,
> Make love's quick pants in Desdemona's arms,
> Give renewed fire to our extincted spirits,
> And bring all Cyprus comfort!—

At which point Desdemona enters, and he continues,

> O, behold!
> The riches of the ship is come on shore!
> You men of Cyprus, let her have your knees.
> Hail to thee, lady! and the grace of heaven,
> Before, behind thee, and on every hand,
> Enwheel thee round!

Cassio is clearly devoted to his commander, and reverently courteous to his commander's wife, but it seems to me that we are entitled to notice the conspicuous difference between the prayers he offers in behalf of each, for one is pagan and one is Christian. As significantly as the recent storm, an omen of the chaos and storm to come, these prayers separate rather than unite husband and wife—though this is certainly not part of Cassio's intention. The prayer for Othello invokes not only Jove but also the four elements: earth, air, fire, and water; while the Christian prayer is no less universal, but distinctly different. We may also be reminded that Cyprus was sacred to Aphrodite (Venus was called the Cyprean Queen), goddess of Love, and we will be struck at how tragic a setting it will be for "the divine Desdemona," who has a supremely Christian, and not a pagan, nature.

But well before this, in the first act, Othello has exhibited that inflated speech and contorted syntax we identify with the most egregious kind of rhetoric and oratory:

> The tyrant custom, most grave senators,
> Hath made the flinty and steel couch of war
> My thrice-driven bed of down: I do agnize
> A natural and prompt alacrity
> I find in hardness.

"Alacrity" is used here in what can only be called an eccentric way, and differently from the way Shakespeare uses it anywhere else. But aside from that, the lines quite obviously instance the sort of "bombast circumstance" Iago mentioned at the start. Lest we think this a momentary lapse, Othello remarks only a few lines later,

> No, when light-wing'd toys
> Of feathered Cupid seel with wanton dullness
> My speculative and offic'd instruments,
> That my disports corrupt and taint my business,
> Let housewives make a skillet of my helm,
> And all indign and base adversities
> Make head against my estimation!

There are puzzles here that only begin with differing lections. The quarto has "foils" for "seel," "active instruments" for "offic'd instruments," and "reputation" for "estimation." The "speculative" instruments may be either the eyes or the meditative mind; the "offic'd" instruments are probably limbs, or those parts of the body obedient to the mind. If "seel" means "blind," as some have thought, it is hard to see how limbs can be blinded, though they can be foiled. If "seel" means "put to sleep," we are presented with a situation in which the supposedly soldierly faculties sleep while the libidinous ones are allowed full play. Presumably Cupid could manage this, but the phraseology is not of the clearest. The passage ends in a sort of boast or defiant taunt: if I should neglect my duties, let housewives domesticate to their "huswifery" the martial emblems of my male profession. And what happens in this play is that in fact the military calling is hideously domesticated; the fury and terror of the field, having no outlet in action, settle into the bedroom, and "honour" is grotesquely fought over, ambiguously won and lost.

Anyway, it is the baroque mode of expression that not only galls Iago (who regards himself as both cunning and as a plain speaker) but is the occasion of his mockery by parody. When the brawl between Cassio and Roderigo occurs, and Othello, having been called to the scene, inquires what happened, Iago declares,

> I do not know. Friends all, but now, even now,
> In quarter, and in terms like bride and groom
> Divesting them for bed; and then, but now—
> As if some planet had unwitted men—
> Swords out, and tilting one at other's breast
> In opposition bloody. I cannot speak
> Any beginning to this peevish odds,
> And would in action glorious I had lost
> Those legs that brought me to a part of it!

I wish to call attention merely to the last two lines of this speech, and suggest that they are nearly ludicrous. Their distorted and silly connection to military glory, their unnecessarily encumbered way of saying the simple "I wish I'd never seen this," their contrived way of blaming his legs for conveying him to the presence of this disagreeable sight, all these are a mockery of what by this time we can recognize as an idiosyncrasy of Othello's mode of expression. Othello is given to the use of the vocative, the apostrophe, all the rhetorical modes and formulas throughout the play.

> O, now for ever
> Farewell the tranquil mind! farewell content!
> Farewell the plumed troop, and the big wars
> That make ambition virtue! O, farewell!
> Farewell the neighing steed and the shrill trump,
> The spirit-stirring drum, th'ear-piercing fife,
> The royal banner, and all quality,
> Pride, pomp, and circumstance of glorious war!
> And, O you mortal engines, whose rude throats
> Th'immortal Jove's dread clamors counterfeit,
> Farewell! Othello's occupation's gone!

Perhaps the first thing that must be said about this speech is that G. Wilson Knight calls it noble; but I think it is a tainted nobility: studied, artful, self-conscious, and almost immediately provocative of a parody by Iago, thus:

> O monstrous world! Take note, take note, O world,
> To be direct and honest is not safe.

This is not the way Iago speaks to anyone else in the play. It should also be noted that Othello, now well advanced in the tragic process of disintegration, here speaks of himself for the first time in the third person, as if he stood apart from himself and were a divided consciousness. This process becomes more and more pronounced as the play continues, and we must return to it in due course. But for the present, we may remark upon the patterned repetitions, the orchestrated luxuriance of military pageantry, the "pomp and circumstance" not of glorious war alone but of this speech. And we may further note the specifically "classical" employment of "engines," *(exeuremata)* and the poetic periphrasis by which the vulgar word "cannon" is avoided (swords and spears being the only weapons suitable for naming, according to epic tradition). Jove is named, and the roar of the unmentionable artillery compared to the thunder of the god. It is hard to feel that this speech's passion is not colored by a self-regard and self-consciousness that a little compromises its "nobility."

There follows almost immediately an interesting, relevant, and curiously disputed passage. Othello insists,

> I'll have some proof. My name, that was as fresh
> As Dian's visage, is now begrimed and black
> As mine own face.

The quarto has "Her name" for "My name," but I think I prefer the folio version, though the choice is not based on anything demonstrable, but simply on my sense of what is wanted here; though it may be added that Othello's earlier repudiation of Cupid is consistent with this identification with Diana. There is, in fact, something very chaste about the way Othello thinks of himself, even within the context of marriage, and this may be one of the reasons he is so vulnerable to Iago. He continues to be concerned with the purity of his own reputation as he compares it to the chastity and whiteness of the moon goddess. The classical, the Roman strain, which dictates that Caesar's wife must be beyond reproach, continues. As does the use of apostrophe:

> Arise, black vengeance, from the hollow hell!
> Yield up, O love, thy crown and hearted throne
> To tyrannous hate! Swell, bosom, with thy fraught,
> For 'tis of aspics' tongues!

And when Iago ventures to test him with, "Patience, I say; your mind perhaps may change," he responds with a nearly Homeric, at least an epic, simile:

> Never, Iago. Like to the Pontic sea,
> Whose icy current and compulsive course
> Ne'er feels retiring ebb, but keeps due on
> To the Propontic and the Hellespont;
> Even so my bloody thoughts, with violent pace
> Shall ne'er look back, ne'er ebb to humble love,
> Till that a capable and wide revenge
> Swallow them up.

It is almost as if he were calling upon classical authority and classical modes of discourse to justify his fury as well as to articulate it. This extended maritime metaphor, with its appropriate qualities of icy coldness, irresistible force, and singleness of direction is all, of course, eminently suitable to his purpose, but we may yet comment that it seems contrived, and that the classicism seems at least as important to Othello as do its local details and the burden of its meaning.

But the meaning, in any case, is persuasive enough for Iago. Having prodded Othello through various stages of torment and desperation, he has by this time brought his commander to his knees, quite literally; and there he joins him in a grotesque travesty of marriage in which the two men exchange vows, Desdemona having been firmly eliminated. And in a curious, half-mocking, half-serious, but sinister parody of Othello's compulsive habit of apostrophe, Iago declares,

> Witness, you ever-burning lights above,
> You elements that clip us round about,
> Witness that here Iago doth give up
> The execution of his wit, hands, heart
> To wronged Othello's service! Let him command,
> And to obey shall be in me remorse,
> What bloody business ever.

It should be apparent that for Othello to think of himself as a classical hero on the one hand, and to think of himself as a pious Christian on the other, involves a painfully uncertain sense of himself, and even of how to "dramatize" himself. It is one of the indices of a very deep perplexity.

Othello's generalship is evidenced in his command of others, his clear impartiality:

Hold your hands,
Both you of my inclining and the rest.

He tries to apply these same methods to Iago's insinuations, and to his own fears:

Think'st thou I'ld make a life of jealousy,
To follow still the changes of the moon
With fresh suspicions? No! To be once in doubt
Is once to be resolved. Exchange me for a goat
When I shall turn the business of my soul
To such exsufflicate and blown surmises,
Matching this inference.

(The *OED* remarks, regarding *exsufflicate,* "apparently an arbitrary formation on Exsufflate"; and the only instance is from this speech.) But of course the swift and objective decisions of a commander are not available to the subjective vacillations of a mind, or the interior torments to which he so much desires to apply them. In all these crises he is concerned with Justice and Honour, both of them conceived as Roman virtues. They are related, moreover, having to do with the preservation of purity from contamination—a species of chastity. And both are matters of public inspection. Justice is established by public evidence and general consent; honour, in both men and women, has to do with reputation, which is publicly assigned. Cassio holds the same Roman regard for Honour, or Reputation, as his commander; and Iago, addressing Othello, adopts the same attitude:

Good name in man and woman, dear my lord,
Is the immediate jewel of their souls.

## Othello Divided Against Himself

Othello's torment and internal strife is like the war of heaven and hell that figures so prominently in the play's language. It is a civil, or an "intestine," struggle, and only in part to be explained by the Christian-Moorish or the Christian-Roman oppositions. It begins with the implantation of the seeds of suspicion in Othello by Iago in act 3. The metaphor of planting a seed which is to bear the evil fruit of death is consistent both with the notion of Iago as Satanic, and with the passive role of Othello. In fact, it is Othello's passivity that in part enrages him, for his passivity is tied to his uncertainty. By the third scene in the act he is terribly divided:

> I think my wife be honest, and think she is not;
> I think that thou art just, and think thou art not.

Honesty, or Honour, and Justice are paralleled here, and the effect of this torment, from Iago's point of view at least, is emasculating, and he keeps pointing to this, not without some inward relish:

> Are you a man?
>
> Would you would bear your fortune like a man!
>
> Good sir, be a man.
>
> A passion most unsuiting such a man—
>
> Marry patience!
>
> Or I shall say y'are all in all in spleen
> And nothing of a man.

The fiendishness of Iago during these scenes consists in provoking Othello's anxieties, frustrations, and furies, and then blaming him for not being able sufficiently to govern them. And Othello's torment arises precisely out of the conflict of the passions he feels and the genuine attempts he makes to govern them. The attempts at government are wholly connected with his role as "Roman" general. Early in the play he was supremely in command of himself and of others. And he never carried his authority with more magisterial effect than with the line, "Keep up your bright swords, for the dew will rust them." The commanding presence who speaks there continues in authority so secure that without discomfort he can show obeisance and obedience to the Duke and senate, though knowing, of course, as everyone seems to know, that in fact they depend wholly upon him. The protocols of mutual courtesy are smoothly and flawlessly observed. What wrecks this seemingly absolute poise is, after all, a change of setting or venue; the field of action shifts from war, where Othello is absolute, to the isle of the Cyprean Queen and the domain of Love in which Othello confesses his inexperience and inadequacy, and where the cynicism of Iago passes for worldly knowledge.

> IAGO: No, let me know;
> And knowing what I am, I know what she shall be.
> OTHELLO: O, thou art wise! 'Tis certain.

Othello has clearly indicated (or as clearly as a muddled text will allow) as early as the first act that he is very nearly disqualified, virtually *hors de combat,* in that field of carnal intimacy in which Iago claims expertise and subtle knowledge. Asking the senate permission to allow Desdemona to accompany him to Cyprus, Othello says,

> Let her have your voice.
> Vouch with me heaven, I therefore beg it not
> To please the palate of my appetite,
> Not to comply with heat—the young affects
> In me defunct—and proper satisfaction;
> But to be free and bounteous to her mind.

There are puzzles here I must pass over, but I would point out that the sort of chastity suggested here obsesses Othello throughout the play, and his mention of Desdemona's mind chimes with her comment, "I saw Othello's visage in his mind." Earlier in the same scene he had said of himself,

> For since these arms of mine had seven years' pith
> Till now some nine moons wasted, they have used
> Their dearest action in the tented field.

If we may take these statements as true and accurate, we must assume that Othello's arms experienced no "dearer" action than warfare from the age of seven until nine months before he speaks here, at which time he declares himself past the age of strong sexual appetite. This means that he has interested himself in no one before Desdemona, and his interest in her is of an uncommon purity. Iago, brilliant opportunist that he is, affects to believe this or not to believe it as suits his various purposes. In his dealings with Brabantio and Roderigo, he strongly affirms the animality of Othello, and associates that animality with rampant sexual energy and with the black skin of a primitive man. Dealing, on the other hand, with Othello, he patiently acknowledges his commander's painful naiveté. Speaking to an utterly credulous Othello, he remarks of his nation's women,

> I know our country disposition well:
> In Venice they do let God see the pranks
> They dare not show their husbands; their best conscience
> Is not to leave't undone, but to keep't unknown.

The torment of division, or disintegration, from which Othello suffers, and which begins in act 3, continues in intensity and divisiveness until he falls into an epileptic seizure, and briefly passes out. One of the definitions of this malady in the *OED* quotes a 1658 text regarding "the Epilepsy that ariseth from the strangling of the Mother," in which "Mother," as it appears in *King Lear*, is hysteria.

> O, how this mother swells up toward my heart!
> Hysterica passio, down, thou climbing sorrow;
> Thine element's below.

We may take it, then, that Othello's epileptic swoon has resulted from his attempt to "strangle" or govern his hysterical passion, and that this is a symbol of his unresolved conflicts. If they are unresolved at this point, they are cruelly revived by Iago almost as soon as Othello comes to. And shortly thereafter we witness an Othello so hideously divided, so totally unmanned, that the spectacle comes as near to seeing protracted and deforming torture on the stage as anything Shakespeare has ever offered.

> OTHELLO: O Iago!
> IAGO: And did you see the handkerchief?
> OTHELLO: Was that mine?
> IAGO: Yours, by this hand! And to see how he prizes the foolish woman your wife! She gave it him, and he hath giv'n it his whore.
> OTHELLO: I would have him nine years a-killing!—A fine woman! a fair woman! a sweet woman!
> IAGO: Nay, you must forget that.
> OTHELLO: Ay, let her rot, and perish, and be damned tonight; for she shall not live. No, my heart is turned to stone; I strike it, and it hurts my hand.—O, the world hath not a sweeter creature! She might lie by an emperor's side and command him tasks.
> IAGO: Nay, that's not your way.
> OTHELLO: Hang her! I do but say what she is. So delicate with her needle!—an admirable musician! O she will sing the savageness out of a bear!—Of so high and plenteous wit and invention!—
> IAGO: She's the worse for all this.
> OTHELLO: O, a thousand, thousand times! And then, of so gentle a condition!
> IAGO: Ay, too gentle.
> OTHELLO: Nay, that's certain. But yet the pity of it Iago! O Iago, the pity of it, Iago!

There are some who find this very nearly unendurable, and it is by no means the end of Othello's exhibition of his inner division. It poisons his interview with Desdemona in the next scene, and is yet present, in a somewhat crazed and hypnotized form, when he enters the last scene of the play.

## Conclusion

When Othello enters the bedchamber in the last scene he has taken upon himself the role of justicer, though by no means for the first time. From the very beginning of the play he was cast as arbiter of all disputes. But here, in his almost dazed condition, he seems to feel himself an agent of the Supreme Law, or of the Roman virtue of Justice. Even in the insane calm of his opening speech he indicates his division from himself, posing in balance the demands of "duty" with his regret at having to perform it, like some deranged Aeneas. He is indeed very nearly demented, and his calm is the more awful for that. It ought to make us shudder as much as, though in a different way from, the spectacle of his symbolic castration. But the evidence of division only begins with this mad attempt at balance. It expresses itself in the patent degeneration of his speech, which already, under the torture of Iago had declined into expletives and groans. Here his vocatives become cries of feebleness:

> But O vain boast!
>
> O ill-starred wench!
>
> O cursed, cursed slave!

This last expression refers to himself, and seems an ironic fulfillment of Brabantio's early prediction:

> For if such actions may have passage free,
> Bondslaves and pagans shall our statesmen be.

The division is expressed in his references to himself again and again in the third person:

> Man but a rush against Othello's breast,
> And he retires. Where should Othello go?

And in response to the question Lodovico asks upon entering, "Where is this rash and most unfortunate man?" Othello responds, "That's he that was Othello. Here I am." There are clearly several ways to read that line. One way is to convey the sense that the speaker knows exactly what he is saying, and means that "Othello," an admirable, competent and decent man, existed in the past, but exists no more, and in his place stands the wreck of man that speaks. Another would suggest that the first part of the line, "That's he that was Othello," would be something like the equivalent of, "He must be talking about me."

In addition, as Wilson Knight has carefully indicated, Othello's long speech beginning, "Behold, I have a weapon," while achieving moments of genuine eloquence, slips suddenly into rant, like music into discord, or, perhaps equally aptly, like order into the chaos of apocalypse that seemed predicted almost from the start. Othello makes feeble attempts to recover himself, as, for example, in finding the concealed sword, but they collapse into nothing, as his speech collapses into raving. And therefore his final speech ought to astonish us as an achievement of unexpected strength and self-command, even as we are astonished to find an unexpected weapon in his possession.

The speech itself is a quite extraordinary piece of oratory. Since he has just been ordered to come away, his very first line is striking: "Soft you! a word or two before you go." Not "before we go," which would have been expected; nor "before I go."

> I have done the state some service, and they know't.
> No more of that.

This cannot be said in extenuation of his crime, since the punishment he will inflict cannot be mitigated. It is the beginning of his request that some balance sheet of his deeds may represent him properly to posterity. For this to be called purely self-regarding vanity is to miss its strong classical, its deliberately Roman component. Fame is desirable, and a proper, even a noble, ambition; and in this speech, with an astonishing summoning of final strength, Othello is exhibiting, without flinching, all his Roman virtues, and some others as well. If he makes no mention of Desdemona here (and he does indeed allude to her) it would be in keeping with the Duke's stoic advice to Brabantio at the beginning of the play:

> When remedies are past, the griefs are ended
> By seeing the worst, which late on hopes depended.

His balance sheet is not merely a plea for justice but a rhetorical feat of extraordinary skill, a speech which, considering all that he has had to face about himself, about Desdemona, about Cassio, about Iago, is nothing short of triumphant in its matched and mated parallelisms, its antiphonal pairings of thesis and antithesis, its decisively Ciceronian patterns of poised and balanced phrases. At no other point in the play does his rhetoric show itself to such advantage, unblemished by contortions or exoticisms. Neither is it merely self-exculpating, nor simply Roman in its courage, if one elects, as I do, for the reading of "base Iudean" rather than "base Indian," and thereby allows Othello, quite consistently with the Christian aspect of his speech, to identify himself with Judas Iscariot, and Desdemona, the pearl he throws away, with Christ. Desdemona not only has proven faultless, but has died refusing to accuse her murderer. And the speaker, as I think, means to convey his complete sense of this. He is therefore committing himself not only to the death by suicide that was the lot of Judas, but to hell and damnation. He had already hinted as much earlier when he said, addressing Desdemona's corpse,

> When we shall meet at compt,
> This look of thine will hurl my soul from heaven,
> And fiends will snatch at it.

In other words, up to this point the speech has united the Roman and the Christian aspects of Othello. And its conclusion will extirpate the Moor, and exhibit in definitive form the absolute division within him. As both defender of the Venetian cause and as the circumcised dog, as both Christian and Muslim, Othello performs the last struggle of his inward life; heaven and hell drive him to his end, and, without hope of redemption in the next life, he asks for an accurate report of this one. The judgment he passes upon himself is absolute and remorseless, though this is not what Eliot meant in charging that he exhibits no remorse. His performance is admittedly theatrical, but it bears so heavy a spiritual penalty, and bears it with such complete consciousness, that the theatrics, I maintain, cease to matter, and he attains a painful but undoubted nobility. His self-inflicted death is the death not only of Judas but of Brutus; it involves both Christian and Roman aspects, which, admittedly, do not sit comfortably together. But that has been part of Othello's drama from the first. And there is a species of oratorical remorse, despite what Eliot says. There are four main items in Othello's balance sheet, and all but the last of them in the past tense. He loved; he was perplexed; he threw the pearl away; but he weeps. His ability to say this, without halting, without inflation or bombast, is in itself an accomplishment that has its spiritual dimension. And his suicide is offered as a Venetian-Christian-Roman victory over guileless trust and ignorance, over the barbarian-pagan innocence of a Moorish slave.

# Chronology

| | |
|---|---|
| 1564 | William Shakespeare born at Stratford-on-Avon to John Shakespeare, a butcher, and Mary Arden. He is baptized on April 26. |
| 1582 | Marries Anne Hathaway in November. |
| 1583 | Daughter Susanna born, baptized on May 26. |
| 1585 | Twins Hamnet and Judith born, baptized on February 2. |
| 1588–90 | Sometime during these years, Shakespeare goes to London, without family. First plays performed in London. |
| 1590–92 | *The Comedy of Errors*, the three parts of *Henry VI*. |
| 1593–94 | Publication of *Venus and Adonis* and *The Rape of Lucrece*, both dedicated to the Earl of Southampton. Shakespeare becomes a sharer in the Lord Chamberlain's company of actors. *The Taming of the Shrew*, *The Two Gentlemen of Verona*, *Richard III*, *Titus Andronicus*. |
| 1595–97 | *Romeo and Juliet*, *Richard II*, *King John*, *A Midsummer Night's Dream*, *Love's Labor's Lost*. |
| 1596 | Son Hamnet dies. Grant of arms to father. |
| 1597 | *The Merchant of Venice*, *Henry IV*, *Part 1*. Purchases New Place in Stratford. |
| 1598–1600 | *Henry IV*, *Part 2*, *As You Like It*, *Much Ado about Nothing*, *Twelfth Night*, *The Merry Wives of Windsor*, *Henry V*, and *Julius Caesar*. Moves his company to the new Globe Theatre. |
| 1601 | *Hamlet*. Shakespeare's father dies, buried on September 8. |
| 1601–2 | *Troilus and Cressida*. |
| 1603 | Death of Queen Elizabeth; James VI of Scotland becomes James I of England; Shakespeare's company becomes the King's Men. |
| 1603–4 | *All's Well That Ends Well*, *Measure for Measure*, *Othello*. |

| | |
|---|---|
| 1605–6 | *King Lear, Macbeth.* |
| 1607 | Marriage of daughter Susanna on June 5. |
| 1607–8 | *Timon of Athens, Antony and Cleopatra, Pericles, Coriolanus.* |
| 1608 | Shakespeare's mother dies, buried on September 9. |
| 1609 | *Cymbeline*, publication of sonnets. Shakespeare's company purchases Blackfriars Theatre. |
| 1610–11 | *The Winter's Tale, The Tempest*. Shakespeare retires to Stratford. |
| 1612–13 | *Henry VIII, Two Noble Kinsmen.* |
| 1616 | Marriage of daughter Judith on February 10. Shakespeare dies at Stratford on April 23. |
| 1623 | Publication of the Folio edition of Shakespeare's plays. |

# Contributors

HAROLD BLOOM, Sterling Professor of the Humanities at Yale University, is the author of *The Anxiety of Influence, Poetry and Repression* and many other volumes of literary criticism. His forthcoming study, *Freud: Transference and Authority*, attempts a full-scale reading of all of Freud's major writings. A MacArthur Prize Fellow, he is general editor of five series of literary criticism published by Chelsea House. During 1987–88, he was appointed Charles Eliot Norton Professor of Poetry at Harvard University.

STANLEY CAVELL is the Walter M. Cabot Professor of Aesthetics and the General Theory of Value at Harvard University. His books include *Must We Mean What We Say?, Pursuits of Happiness: The Hollywood Comedy of Remarriage*, and *The Claim of Reason*.

SUSAN SNYDER, Professor of English at Swarthmore College, is the editor of Sylvester's *DuBartas* and the author of *The Comic Matrix of Shakespeare's Tragedies*.

STEPHEN GREENBLATT, Class of 1932 Professor of English at the University of California, Berkeley, is an editor of the journal *Representations*. He is the author of *Sir Walter Raleigh: The Renaissance Man and His Roles* and *Renaissance Self-Fashioning: From More to Shakespeare*.

MARK ROSE is Professor of English at the University of California at Santa Barbara. His books include *Heroic Love: Studies in Sidney and Spencer, Shakespearian Design*, and *Spencer's Art*.

CAROL THOMAS NEELY teaches English at Illinois State University. She is coeditor of *The Woman's Part: Feminist Criticism of Shakespeare*, and the author of *Broken Nuptials in Shakespeare's Plays*.

PATRICIA PARKER, Professor of English and Comparative Literature at the University of Toronto, is the author of *Inescapable Romance*. She is the coeditor of *Lyric Poetry: Beyond New Criticism*, *Shakespeare and the Question of Theory*, and *Literary Theory and Renaissance Texts*.

ANTHONY HECHT is Professor of English at Georgetown University. His many books include *Millions of Strange Shadows*, *The Venetian Vespers*, and *Obbligati: Essays in Criticism*.

# Bibliography


Adamson, Jane. *Othello as Tragedy: Some Problems of Judgment and Feeling*. Cambridge: Cambridge University Press, 1980.

Adamson, W. A. "Unpinned or Undone?: Desdemona's Critics and the Problem of Sexual Innocence." *Shakespeare Studies* 13 (1980): 169–86.

Bayley, John. *The Characters of Love*, 125–201. New York: Basic Books, 1960.

Bonnard, G. "Are Othello and Desdemona Innocent or Guilty?" *English Studies* 30 (1949): 175–84.

Boose, Linda. "Othello's Handkerchief: 'The Recognizance and Pledge of Love.' " *English Literary Renaissance* 5(1975): 360–74.

Bradley, A. C. *Shakespearean Tragedy*. 2d. ed. London: Macmillan, 1924.

Bullough, Geoffrey. *Narrative and Dramatic Sources of Shakespeare*. London: Routledge & Kegan Paul, 1973.

Bulman, James C. *The Heroic Idiom of Shakespearean Tragedy*. Newark: University of Delaware Press, 1985.

Burke, Kenneth. "*Othello:* An Essay to Illustrate a Method." *The Hudson Review* 4 (1951–52): 165–203.

Colie, Rosalie. *Shakespeare's Living Art*. Princeton, N.J.: Princeton University Press, 1974.

Cook, Ann Jennalie. "The Design of Desdemona: Doubt Raised and Resolved." *Shakespeare Studies* 13 (1980): 187–96.

Dickes, Robert. "Desdemona: An Innocent Victim?" *American Imago* 27 (1970): 279–97.

Eliot, T. S. "Shakespeare and the Stoicism of Seneca." In *Selected Essays*, 110–11. New York: Harcourt, Brace, Jovanovich, 1950.

Elliot, G. R. *Flaming Minister: A Study of Othello*. Durham, N.C.: Duke University Press, 1953.

Empson, William. *The Structure of Complex Words*. London: Chatto & Windus, 1951.

Felperin, Howard. *Shakespearean Representation*. Princeton, N.J.: Princeton University Press, 1977.

Fiedler, Leslie. *The Stranger in Shakespeare*. New York: Stein & Day, 1972.

Flatter, Richard. *The Moor of Venice*. London: William Heinemann, 1950.

Gardner, Helen. "The Noble Moor." *Proceedings of the British Academy* 41 (1955): 189–205.

———. "*Othello:* A Retrospect, 1900–67." In *Shakespeare Survey* 21 (1968): 1–11.
Garner, S. N. "Shakespeare's Desdemona." *Shakespeare Studies* 9 (1976): 233–52.
Gohlke, Madelon. " 'I wooed thee with my sword': Shakespeare's Tragic Paradigms." In *The Woman's Part: Feminist Criticism of Shakespeare*, edited by Carolyn Ruth Swift Lenz, Gayle Greene and Carol Thomas Neely. Urbana: University of Illinois Press, 1980.
———. " 'All that is spoke is marred': Language and Consciousness in *Othello*." *Women's Studies* 9 (1981–82): 157–76.
Granville-Barker, H. *Prefaces to Shakespeare*. London: Batsford, 1958.
Greene, Gayle. " 'This that you call love': Sexual and Social Tragedy in *Othello*." *Journal of Women's Studies in Literature* 1 (1979): 16–32.
Heilman, R. B. *Magic in the Web*. Lexington: University of Kentucky Press, 1956.
Hunter, G. K. "Othello and Colour Prejudice." *The Proceedings of the British Academy* 53 (1967): 139–63. Reprinted in *Dramatic Identities and Cultural Tradition*. New York: Barnes & Noble, 1978.
Hyman, Stanley Edgar. *Iago: Some Approaches to the Illusion of his Motivation*. New York: Atheneum, 1970.
Jeffrey, David L. and Patrick Grant. "Reputation in *Othello*." *Shakespeare Studies* 6 (1970): 197–208.
Kahn, Coppélia. *Man's Estate: Masculine Identity in Shakespeare*. Berkeley: University of California Press, 1981.
Kirsch, Arthur. *Shakespeare and the Experience of Love*, 10–39. Cambridge: Cambridge University Press, 1981.
Kirschbaum, Leo. "The Modern Othello." *ELH* 11 (1944): 283–96.
Knight, G. Wilson. *The Wheel of Fire*, 107–31. 1930. Reprint. London: Oxford University Press, 1946.
Leavis, F. R. *The Common Pursuit*. London: Chatto & Windus, 1952.
Mason, H. A. *Shakespeare's Tragedies of Love*. New York: Barnes & Noble, 1970.
Matteo, Gino J. *Shakespeare's Othello: The Study and the Stage, 1604–1904*. Salzburg, Austria: Institut für Englische Sprache und Literatur, Universität Salzburg, 1974.
Neill, Michael. "Changing Places in *Othello*." *Shakespeare Survey* 37 (1984): 115–31.
Nevo, Ruth. *Tragic Form in Shakespeare*. Princeton: Princeton University Press, 1972.
Rosenberg, Marvin. *The Masks of Othello*. Berkeley: University of California Press, 1961.
Rossiter, A. P. *Angel with Horns*. New York: Theatre Arts Books, 1961.
Snow, Edward. "Sexual Anxiety and the Male Order of Things in *Othello*." *English Literary Renaissance* 10, no. 3 (1980): 385–411.
Wheeler, Richard P. " 'And my loud crying still': The Sonnets, *The Merchant of Venice*, and *Othello*." In *Shakespeare's Rough Magic: Renaissance Essays for C. L. Barber*. Edited by Peter Erickson and Coppélia Kahn. Newark: University of Delaware Press, 1985.
Zacha, Richard. "Iago and the *Commedia dell'arte*." *Arlington Quarterly* 2 (1969): 98–116.

# Acknowledgments

"Epistemology and Tragedy: A Reading of *Othello*" by Stanley Cavell from *Hypocrisy, Illusion and Evasion, Daedalus* 108, no. 3 (Summer 1979), © 1979 by the American Academy of Arts and Sciences. Reprinted by permission.

"Beyond Comedy: *Othello*" (originally entitled "Beyond Comedy: *Romeo and Juliet* and *Othello*") by Susan Snyder from *The Comic Matrix of Shakespeare's Tragedies*, by Susan Snyder, © 1979 by Princeton University Press. Reprinted by permission of Princeton University Press.

"The Improvisation of Power" by Stephen Greenblatt from *Renaissance Self-Fashioning: From More to Shakespeare* by Stephen Greenblatt, © 1980 by the University of Chicago. Reprinted by permission of the author and the University of Chicago Press.

"Othello's Occupation: Shakespeare and the Romance of Chivalry" by Mark Rose from *English Literary Renaissance* 15, no. 3 (Autumn 1985), © 1985 by *English Literary Renaissance*. Reprinted by permission of *English Literary Renaissance*.

"Women and Men in *Othello*" by Carol Thomas Neely from *Broken Nuptials in Shakespeare's Plays* by Carol Thomas Neely, © 1985 by Yale University. Reprinted by permission of Yale University Press.

"Shakespeare and Rhetoric: 'Dilation' and 'Delation' in *Othello*" by Patricia Parker from *Shakespeare and the Question of Theory*, edited by Patricia Parker and Geoffrey H. Hartman, © 1985 by Methuen & Co. Ltd. Reprinted by permission of Methuen & Co.

"Othello" by Anthony Hecht from *Obbligati: Essays in Criticism* by Anthony Hecht, © 1986 by Anthony E. Hecht. Reprinted by permission of Atheneum Publishers, Inc.

# Index

narrative—although not of course the contradictions that drive the narrative—is resolved.

## VII

Iago's diabolism is of course only metaphorical. Shakespeare is exploring a secular equivalent to demonic possession, showing how a terrible misapprehension can take control of a normally rational mind. *Othello,* in which there are neither ghosts, soothsayers, witches, nor supernatural prodigies, is one of the most secular of Shakespeare's tragedies. Nevertheless, it is significant that the word "devil" occurs in its various forms more often here than in any other Shakespeare play. The word "faith," too, is prominent whether it is used casually as in Iago and Cassio's discussion of Bianca where it occurs repeatedly as a mild expletive (4.1) or whether it is used portentously as in Othello's tremendous oath, "My life upon her faith" (1.3.294). What Shakespeare is doing in this play is appropriating spiritual conceptions, turning them into metaphors for secular experiences. But metaphors work two ways. If *Othello* incorporates a process of demystification, the assimilation of the supernatural to the natural world, it also incorporates the antithetical movement. The story may not literally be the temptation and fall of man from faith, but the play is not purely domestic tragedy either. An interpretation may legitimately stress either the process of naturalization or the way the domestic drama suggests events of cosmic significance. Like all of Shakespeare's work, *Othello* is implicated in the Renaissance system of analogical thought in which the realms of matter and spirit are not yet wholly divided and distinguished. Thus the play can be at once domestic and cosmic, secular and supernatural.

*Othello* is fascinating as a historical document because of the way it inscribes a transitional moment in Western culture. In it we can almost see the supernatural realm receding. The feudal world of honor, fidelity, and service is becoming the bourgeois world of property and contractual relations. Heroic tragedy is turning into domestic tragedy. It was Shakespeare's fortune to partake of two worlds without belonging completely to either. Shakespeare's myriad-mindedness—the quality that Norman Rabkin speaks of as complementarity—has much to do with this particular historical situation, as does his endless self-consciousness, the metadramatic aspect of his plays that has been emphasized by Sigurd Burckhardt and James Calderwood.

We can locate Shakespeare's historical situation with some precision by observing that his friend and colleague Ben Jonson, a man less than ten years younger than Shakespeare, belongs much more to the new era.

Whereas Shakespeare fuses and blends the spiritual and the secular, the realms of honor and commerce, Jonson uses comic irony to create distinctions. The spectacularly blasphemous opening of *Volpone*—a play like *Othello* set in the commercial city of Venice—makes the point.

> Good morning to the day; and next, my gold!
> Open the shrine that I may see my saint.
> Hail the world's soul, and mine! More glad than is
> The teeming earth to see the longed-for sun
> Peep through the horns of the celestial Ram,
> Am I, to view thy splendor darkening his;
> That lying here, amongst my other hoards,
> Show'st like a flame by night, or like the day
> Struck out of chaos, when all darkness fled
> Unto the center.

Here the Renaissance system of correspondence between matter and spirit, microcosm and macrocosm, is used against itself to expose the gap between traditional values and the realities of the marketplace and to suggest the emptying out of spiritual significance from the world.

Jonson typically pokes fun at magicians, monsters, and fairy queens. Concerned with verisimilitude and poetic justice, his plays look forward in a way that Shakespeare's, with their marvels, anachronisms, and freedoms of time and place, do not. His attitude toward chivalric romanticism is also different from Shakespeare's. In *Prince Henry's Barriers,* the masque that Jonson wrote in connection with the Prince of Wales's first bearing arms in January 1610, Henry is cast as the reviver of chivalry. The masque begins with the Lady of the Lake praising James's court as greater than Arthur's but lamenting the decay of chivalry which is represented by the scene, the ruined House of Chivalry. Arthur appears and prophesies the advent of a knight who will restore chivalry, whereupon Merlin rises from his tomb to reveal Prince Henry, discovered with his companions in arms in a new scene representing St. George's Portico, where knighthood now lives. In a long speech Merlin lectures the Prince on English history, emphasizing industriousness, peaceability, and other values that are distinctly not chivalric. Most interesting, Merlin says that Henry will not seek to emulate the deeds of "antique knights" by thinking to rescue ladies from giants or to do battle with a score of men at once.

> These were bold stories of our Arthur's age;
> But here are other acts; another stage

> And scene appears; it is not since as then:
> No giants, dwarfs or monsters here, but men.

The arts of the modern hero must be to govern and give laws and to preserve the peace whenever possible.

The matter-of-factness incorporated in the apparently romantic and chivalric pageant of *Prince Henry's Barriers* may remind us of the similar quality in Francis Beaumont's *The Knight of the Burning Pestle*, probably performed three years earlier in 1607. Here too we are in a world of men, a world drained of the supernatural and marvelous. Like Jonson in the comedies, Beaumont uses comedy to make distinctions between realms that Shakespeare characteristically blends. Shakespeare's Hal fuses the language of the marketplace and that of the field of honor, speaking of Hotspur as his factor to purchase glorious deeds for him wholesale. Beaumont disjoins the two realms, gaining comic mileage by placing Hotspur's "bright honor" speech in Rafe the grocer's man's mouth and then by placing Rafe and his chivalric posturings in a world in which innkeepers expect to be paid and servants to be tipped. In this unromantic place things are simply what they are, and the comedy ridicules Rafe's attempt to transvalue them by renaming forests and heaths "deserts," horses "palfreys," and by referring to females as either "fair lady" or "distressed damsel" depending upon whether they have their desires or not.

At this point *Don Quixote*, which may have influenced both Beaumont and Jonson, virtually demands to be mentioned. I referred to Cervantes earlier in order to distinguish between his novelistic exploration of the romanticizing imagination and Shakespeare's play in which the protagonist's romanticism is not perfectly demarcated from the general world of the narrative. Published in 1605, a year after *Othello* was performed, *Don Quixote* marks a cultural watershed, the emergence of what Michel Foucault calls the classical episteme. In the Renaissance, Foucault suggests, the principle of resemblance plays a constitutive role in knowledge. The Renaissance conceives a universe of magical correspondences. From this point of view the cosmos is a single vast text and knowledge is a form of interpretation, a matter of reading the mystic signatures written in things. There is finally no difference between language and nature, authority and observation. In *Don Quixote*, however, the bond between words and things has been severed. The Don seeks to reestablish a world of magical resemblances; his entire journey is a quest for similitudes. But the world he inhabits is one in which things are simply what they are, one in which flocks and serving girls are not subject to the transmutation of language.

The Renaissance cosmos has dissolved. In its place the empire of fact is emerging and language is retreating into a special domain, literature, with only an indirect relationship to the world in the neoclassical doctrines of representation and verisimilitude.

It is indicative of the importance of chivalry as a locus for the contradictions of Renaissance culture that such a crucial text as *Don Quixote* should take the form of a negation of chivalric romance. While the chivalric revival of the sixteenth century helped to obscure some of the social and intellectual contradictions of the period, it also contributed to them, raising, as it were, the level of tension by a notch. We can note that in its nostalgia the chivalric revival as a way of possessing the past, of turning chivalry into property. To turn honor literally into property, as the sale of honors did, or to portray merchants and tradesmen in heroic postures, as the bourgeois hero tales did, was to approach the breaking point. In Jonson, Beaumont, and above all in Cervantes, the contradictions of the late Renaissance snap into laughter. *Don Quixote* in particular prefigures the bourgeois civilization of the later seventeenth and eighteenth centuries in which the romance becomes the novel and the emblematic theater of the world, Shakespeare's theater, becomes the illusionistic theater of scenes and stage properties, the theater of things.

## VIII

But what of Shakespeare, whose sensibility is perhaps as close to that of Spenser as to Jonson? Shakespeare, who came to maturity in the 1580s at the height of the Elizabethan revival of chivalry, was not ready to write antiromances like *Don Quixote* or *The Knight of the Burning Pestle*. He was, I think, still too deeply possessed by the absolute world of fidelity. He could write about the death of chivalry or the corruption of chivalry but he could not distance himself sufficiently from its imaginative claims to burlesque it. As a principal shareholder in London's most successful theatrical company and an energetic accumulator of wealth in Stratford and London, Shakespeare evidently participated in the new ethos of the marketplace. But he was also still something of a romantic, even if an unillusioned one.

I suggested earlier that we might think of *Othello* as a play in which Shakespeare recapitulates his own earlier representations of the absolute world of chivalry and that we might regard Iago, the cunning artist of tragedy, as at least in part a representation of Shakespeare himself. Iago is not bourgeois man—that creature had not, so to speak, been thought in 1604. Nevertheless, he is a figure in which the age could find something like the bourgeois cast of mind, together with the multitude of fears and desires that it aroused, made manifest. But Iago is not simply the pragmatist and materialist that he seems to take himself to be. Why should he want to destroy Othello? Iago and Othello are reciprocal figures, part of the same—to use Burke's word—fascination. Just as Othello is possessed by Iago, so Iago is from the beginning of the play possessed by Othello. But though Iago succeeds in destroying the Moor and Desdemona as well, he does not, we might say, succeed in exorcising the spirit they embody. Desdemona remains a miracle of fidelity to the end, and Othello, released from the demi-devil's snares, dies reasserting his allegiance to his heroic self.

True enough; yet to conclude our discussion on this romantic note of sustained fidelity and reasserted heroism misrepresents the tenor of Shakespeare's play. Othello may be an honorable murderer but he is a murderer nonetheless, and at the story's end both Desdemona and the Moor are dead. The world of *Othello* is not that of the novel, the characteristic genre of bourgeois civilization, but neither is it that of Elizabethan romance. *Othello* represents an intermediate moment in cultural development and an intermediate form, tragedy. Romance incorporates certainties, absolute opposites of good and evil. Tragedy subverts, deconstructs, certainties and absolutes, or, as Fredric Jameson puts it, tragedy rebukes romance. What Shakespeare has done in *Othello* is to convert the material of Elizabethan romance into tragedy.

Tragedy involves *katharsis:* purging, cleansing, exorcising. The scapegoats of this particular tragic sacrifice are Desdemona and Othello, figures of an exquisite and dangerous romantic beauty. The high priest is Iago, who draws us as audience into dynamic engagement with his purposes, mobilizing destructive emotions that we may not wish to acknowledge. We participate with Iago in splitting open the absolutes of Othello's martial pastoral. We assist in his project of driving the romance hero and his lady out of the world, of torturing Othello and Desdemona to death. Like Othello, we too are in a sense possessed. But because this is theater we are simultaneously dispossessed. Iago engages our rapaciousness, jealousy, and fear, but he also allows us to alienate ourselves from those ungentle emotions, projecting them onto him. Thus he too becomes a scapegoat. Protagonist and antagonist cancel each other out. We are left at the end with neither a reassertion of an old world nor a prefiguration of a new one, but a mere vacancy, or, rather, a tableau of corpses and a disconcerting promise that Iago too will be tortured.

# Women and Men in *Othello*

*Carol Thomas Neely*

> *What should such a fool*
> *Do with so good a woman?*
> *Othello*, 5.2.234–35

Relations between love, sexuality, and marriage are under scrutiny in *Othello*, as in the comedies, problem plays, and *Hamlet*. In more extreme form than in the problem plays, we see here the idealization and degradation of sexuality, the disintegration of male authority and the loss of female power, the isolation of men and women, and the association of sexual consummation with death. The festive comedies conclude with the anticipation of fertile marriage beds. The problem comedies achieve their resolutions with the help of midpoint bedtricks. The marriage bed is at the very heart of the tragedy of *Othello;* offstage but dramatically the center of attention in the first scene and again in the first scene of the second act, it is literally and symbolically at the center of the last scene and is explicitly hidden from sight at the conclusion. Whether the marriage is consummated, when it is consummated, and what the significance of this consummation is for Othello and Desdemona have all been an important source of debate about the play. Throughout its critical history, *Othello*, like the other problem plays, has generated passionate and radically conflicting responses—responses that are invariably tied to the critics' emotional responses to the characters and to the gender relations in the play. Othello, Iago, and Desdemona have been loved and loathed, defended and attacked, judged and exonerated by critics just as they are by characters within the play.

---

From *Broken Nuptials in Shakespeare's Plays*.  Yale University Press, 1985.

"Almost damned in a fair wife" is Leslie Fiedler's alternate title for his chapter on *Othello* in *The Stranger in Shakespeare*. In it he asserts of the women in the play: "Three out of four, then, [are] weak, or treacherous, or both." Thus he seconds Iago's misogyny and broadens the attack on what Leavis has called "The sentimentalist's *Othello*," the traditional view of the play held by Coleridge, Bradley, Granville-Barker, Knight, Bayley, Gardner, and many others. These "Othello critics," as I shall call them, accept Othello at his own high estimate. They are enamored of his "heroic music," affirm his love, and, like him, are overwhelmed by Iago's diabolism, to which they devote much of their analysis. Like Othello, they do not always argue rationally or rigorously for their views and so are vulnerable to attacks on their romanticism or sentimentality. Reacting against these traditionalists, "Iago critics" (Eliot, Empson, Kirschbaum, Rossiter, and Mason, as well as Fiedler and Leavis) take their cues from Iago. Like him, they are attracted to Othello, unmoved by his rhetoric, and eager to "set down the pegs that make this music." They attack Othello at his most vulnerable point, his love. They support their case by quoting Iago's estimates of Othello; they emphasize Iago's realism and "honesty" while priding themselves on their own. Their realism or cynicism gives them, with Iago, an apparent invulnerability. But, like "Othello critics," they share the bias and blindness of the character whose perspective they adopt. Most damagingly, both groups of critics, like both Othello and Iago, badly misunderstand and misrepresent the women in the play.

Iago critics implicitly demean Desdemona, for if Othello's character and love are called into question, then her love for him loses its justification and validity. Explicitly they have little to say about her. Othello critics idealize her along with the hero, but, like him, they have a tendency to see her as an object. The source of her sainthood seems a passivity verging on catatonia: "Desdemona is helplessly passive. She can do nothing whatever. She cannot retaliate even in speech; no, not even in silent feeling. . . . She is helpless because her nature is infinitely sweet and her love absolute. . . . Desdemona's suffering is like that of the most loving of dumb creatures tortured without cause by the being he adores." Iago critics, finding the same trait, condemn Desdemona for it. "But the damage to her symbolic value is greater when we see her passively *leaving everything to Heaven*. She ought in a sense to have *embodied* Heaven, given us a human equivalent that would 'make sense' of Heaven. For this task she had the wrong sort of purity." When Desdemona is credited with activity, she is condemned for that, too; she is accused of being domineering, of using witchcraft, of rebelliousness, disobedience, wantonness. Although discussion of her has frequently been an afterthought to the analysis of the men, recently she has been the focus of a number of studies. Both Othello and Iago critics tend to see good versus evil as the play's central theme, Othello versus Iago as the play's central conflict, and hence, the major tragedies as its most important context.

A third group of "Iago-Othello critics," including Kenneth Burke, Arthur Kirsch, Stephen Greenblatt, Stanley Cavell, Edward Snow, and Richard Wheeler, elide the divisions between the first two groups and view the play from a perspective more like my own. They see Othello and Iago as closely identified with each other; they are "two parts of a single motive—related not as the halves of a sphere, but each implicit in the other." They find the source of the tragedy in Iago-Othello's anxieties regarding women, sexuality, and marriage—anxieties that are universal and generated by underlying social or psychological paradigms. Like Iago-Othello, these critics find the tragedy inevitable and locate its "cause" in an impersonal, implacable agency outside of the protagonists: for Burke, this "cause" is the "disequilibrium of monogamistic love"; for Kirsch, it is "the polarization of erotic love," with its psychological and theological roots; for Greenblatt, it is ambivalent Christian views of marital sexuality as chaste and adulterous; for Snow, it is "the male order of things," the patriarchal society that represses male sexuality and suppresses female sexuality at the behest of the superego; for Cavell, it is universal (male) fears of impotence and deflowering, and of mortality; for Wheeler, it is the conflict among male autonomy, female sexuality, and nurturing femininity. These critics do not ignore or sanctify Desdemona; nor do they condemn her explicitly. All emphasize her active, loving, passionate sensuality and extol her worth. An effect of their focus is, however, that she, more than Iago, becomes the cause of Othello's destruction; it is her relaxed, frank, sexuality and the passionate response it arouses in Othello which generate the tragedy. These critics show how Desdemona's virtues catalyze Othello's sexual anxieties, but they fail to emphasize enough that she has the potential to provide a cure for them.

With this third group of critics, I argue that the play's central theme is love—specifically marital love—that its central conflict is between the men and the women, and that contexts as illuminating as the tragedies are its source, Cinthio's *Gli Hecatommithi* and Shakespeare's preceding comedies. Within *Othello* it is Emilia who most explicitly speaks to this theme, recognizes this central conflict, and inherits from the heroines of comedy the role of potential mediator of it. She is dramatically and symbolically the play's fulcrum. It is as an Emilia critic, then, that I should like to approach the play, hoping to perceive it with something akin to her clear-sighted passion.

*Gli Hecatommithi* could have provided *Othello* with its theme and organizing principle as well as with its plot. The battle of the sexes in marriage is its central motif and dominates the frame, subject matter, and arrangement of the tales. In the introduction the company debates whether harmony can be achieved in marriage. Ponzio denies this, supporting his view with platitudes that Iago would relish: "Better bury a woman than marry her"; "For there to be peace between husband and wife, the husband must be deaf and the wife blind." Fabio, the group's leader, asserts instead that "the only rational love is that which has marriage as its goal, and that this is the quiet of true and wise lovers, coupled together, cooling their amorous flames with sage discourse and in legitimate union." *Othello* similarly presents marriage as either potentially strife-ridden or harmonious. In *Gli Hecatommithi* the debate continues in the tales, and in the Third Decade it is intensified by the inflammatory subject matter—the infidelity of husbands and wives. The seventh tale, the source of *Othello,* is a rebuttal of the sixth, in which a husband discovers his wife's infidelity and, as the company judges, "most prudently" *(prudentissimamente)* arranges to have her "accidentally" drowned. In the eighth tale, a contrast to the two preceding it, harmony supersedes warfare. A wife forgives her unfaithful husband and wins him back, behaving with a "prudence" *(la prudenza)* exactly opposite to the behavior of the husbands in tales six and seven. *Othello* similarly rings changes on the theme of male and female in a series of parallel and contrasting couples—Desdemona / Othello, Emilia / Iago, Bianca / Cassio—along with fantasy couples—Roderigo / Desdemona, Cassio / Desdemona, Othello / Emilia. Throughout the tales of the Third Decade it is most often the men who intensify the conflicts, practicing infidelity or taking revenge on wives they suspect of infidelity; the wives, even when wronged, often succeed in mending the relationships. The men in *Othello* similarly seek revenge; the women similarly seek to secure harmonious relationships but fail to do so.

Their predecessors in this task are the heroines of Shakespearean comedy, to which *Othello* shows pervasive and profound resemblances. Though it is almost always assumed that *Othello* is dominated by a tightly meshed plot, the play seems, like many of the comedies, loosely plotted, held together by theme. The conflicts introduced in the first act between Desdemona and her father and between Venetians and Turks evaporate before they are under way exactly as do those between Hermia and Egeus in *Midsummer Night's Dream* and between Duke Frederick and Duke Senior in *As You Like It.* As in the comedies, these early plot developments are presented in a flat, compressed way; they seem almost an excuse to get the characters to the woods or to Cyprus where the play's real conflicts emerge. Iago plots the remainder of the play; but his scheme is slight, repetitive, and flawed. It has been found lacking in both motive (like Rosalind's plot in *As You Like It*) and goal (like Don John's plot in *Much Ado about Nothing*), and although the play's increasing intensity is undeniable, there is little actual plot development between the end of the first phase of the temptation scene (3.3.275) [All *Othello* citations are to the Arden Shakespeare edition, ed. M. R. Ridley] and the attempt on Cassio's life in act 5. Iago's destruction of Othello, like Rosalind's education of Orlando, is not merely linear. Both are continually starting over; they are repeated variations on opposite themes: Iago works to induce fantasy and Rosalind to dispel it. Neither entirely succeeds. Iago's plot, like those of the comedies, rests on coincidence and absurdity. The handkerchief is like the givens of the comedies—the fairy juice, the caskets, the disguises, the identical twins; it is trivial and ridiculous but, as I shall show, symbolically all-important. The play proceeds as much by a clash of attitudes, viewpoints, and sexes as by plot developments.

Structure, too, imitates that of the pastoral comedies in its movement from an urban center to an isolated retreat, with resultant intensity, freedom, breakdown, and interaction among disparate characters. Though Othello refers to Cyprus as a "town of war," once the threats of Turks and the storm have lifted, it is instead Venus's isle, a place for celebration—relaxation, drinking, eating (dinner arrangements are a frequent topic of conversation here as in Arden), flirting, sleeping, lovemaking. In the comedies, the potential corruption of these activities is suggested in witty banter, songs, comic simile and metaphor; in *Othello*, this corruption becomes literal.

The play is a terrifying completion of the comedies. In them, realism and romanticism, lust and desire, heterosexual and homosexual bonds, male and female power are held in precarious balance. The men's idealism, misogyny, foolishness, and anxiety are mocked, transformed, and dispelled—"laugh[ed] to scorn" (*As You Like It*, 4.2.19)—by disguises and mock deaths, by parodied or aborted nuptials, by delayed or deceitful consummations. The women, through their "high and plenteous wit and invention" (*Othello*, 4.1.185), transform the men from foolish lovers into—we trust—sensible husbands, and at the end submit to their control. Although "The cuckoo then, on every tree, / Mocks married men," (*Love's Labor's Lost*, 5.2.896–97), the mockery grounds love without seriously threatening it. The comedies' relaxed incorporation of marital sexuality is evident in their endings, which look forward to fruitful, harmonious marital consummation—in the fairy-blessed beds of the *Midsummer Night's Dream* couples; the rewon beds of Bassanio and Portia, Gratiano and Nerissa in *Merchant of Venice;* the "well-deserved bed" of Silvius and the rest in *As You Like It*. But in *Othello*, the marriage has taken place before the play begins, and its consummation may already be under way, imaged by Iago as a theft, a violent attack. In the play, women's wit is constrained, their power over men is lost, and the men are transformed downward—"to be now and now a sensible man, by and by a fool, and presently a beast" (2.3.296–97). The men's profound anxieties and murderous fantasies cannot be restrained by the women's affection, wit, and shrewishness. The play ends as it began, in a world of men—political, loveless, undomesticated.

The men in *Othello* extend and darken the anxieties of the comedy heroes. They are, in Emilia's words, "murderous coxcombs" (5.2.234). Three out of the five attempt murder; five out of the five are foolish and vain. Roderigo, most obviously a coxcomb, shows in exaggerated fashion the dangerous combination of romanticism and misogyny and the dissociation of love and sex that all the men share. He is a parody of the conventional Petrarchan lover: love is a "torment," death a "physician" (1.3.308–9), Desdemona "full of most blest condition" (2.1.247), and consummation of their relationship securely impossible. Yet he easily accepts Desdemona's supposed adultery and the necessity of Cassio's murder; his casual cynicism comes to outdo Iago's: " 'Tis but a man gone" (5.1.10). The other men have similarly divided and possessive views of women. Brabantio shifts abruptly from protective affection for the chaste Desdemona—"of spirit / So still and quiet, that her motion / Blush'd at her self" (1.3.94–96)—to physical revulsion from the assertive sexuality revealed by her elopement—"I had rather to adopt a child than get it" (1.3.191). Cassio's divided view is more conventionally accommodated. He idealizes the "divine Desdemona," flirting courteously and cautiously with her and rejecting Iago's insinuations about her sexuality; this side of women is left to Bianca, who is a "monkey" and a "fitchew" and is used and degraded for it. Othello's conflict regarding women is more profound, and the other men's solutions are not open to him. Because of his marriage and his integrity, he cannot, like Roderigo, assert Desdemona's chastity and corruptibility simultaneously; like Cassio, direct his divided emotions toward different objects; or, like Brabantio, disown the problem.

Othello's shifts from the idealization of women to their degradation are "extravagant and wheeling" (1.1.136). Iago is the catalyst, but Othello makes his task easy. At the play's start, Othello's idealistic love, like that of the comedy heroes, needs some realistic grounding in the facts of sex.

For Othello, sex is secondary and potentially either frivolous or debilitating and in conflict with his soldier's duty;

no, when light-wing'd toys,
And feather'd Cupid, foils with wanton dullness
My speculative and active instruments,
That my disports corrupt and taint my business,
Let housewives make a skillet of my helm,
And all indign and base adversities
Make head against my reputation!
(1.3.268–74)

Marriage and consummation naturally pose a threat to this idealistic love. Othello's greeting on Cyprus suggests his preference for a perpetually unconsummated courtship:

If it were now to die,
'Twere now to be most happy, for I fear
My soul hath her content so absolute,
That not another comfort, like to this
Succeeds in unknown fate.
(2.1.189–93)

In response Desdemona asserts instead quotidian joys:

The heavens forbid
But that our loves and comforts should increase,
Even as our days do grow.

Perhaps she, like Rosalind or Viola or the ladies in *Love's Labor's Lost*, might have tempered Othello's idealism, his need for absolute, unchanging love. Instead, it is nudged by Iago into its antithesis—contempt for women, disgust at sexuality, terror of cuckoldry, the preference for literal death over metaphorical "death." The acceptance of cuckoldry and sexuality found in the comedies—"as horns are odious, they are necessary" (*As You Like It*, 3.3.49–50)—is impossible for Othello. Instead he turns Petrarchan imagery against Desdemona—"O thou black weed, why art so lovely fair?" (*Othello*, 4.2.69)—praising and damning her simultaneously. His conflicts are resolved, his needs to idealize and degrade her to maintain their love intact are momentarily reconciled only when he kills her, performing a sacrifice which is also a murder.

Iago, though primarily the manipulator of these conflicts in the other men, is also the victim of his own. His cynical generalizations are, like those of Jaques, the parody and inverse of the romantics' claims; they are self-conscious, defensive, self-aggrandizing, and divorced from reality: "My muse labours / And thus she is deliver'd" (2.1.127–28). Like the other men, he accepts generalizations—especially generalizations about women—as true, provided they are "apt and of great credit" (2.1.282), "probable, and palpable to thinking" (1.2.76). Like the others, he is careful not to contaminate his fantasies about women with facts. Roderigo does not court Desdemona in person, Othello does not immediately confront Desdemona and Cassio with his suspicions, and Iago never tries to ascertain whether or not Emilia is unfaithful.

In fact—like Don John and Parolles—he has little contact with the women in the play. He is at ease in act 2 engaging Desdemona in witty banter, but he is subdued and almost speechless in act 4 when confronted with her misery and fidelity. Treating Emilia with casual contempt throughout, he is astounded by her exposure of him in the last scene. Like Brabantio, Iago assumes that "consequence" will "approve" his "dream" (2.3.58) and ignores evidence to the contrary.

Even protected as it is from reality, Iago's cynicism/misogyny has cracks just as Othello's idealism does. He has a grudging admiration for and envy of Desdemona's "blest condition," Othello's "constant, noble loving, nature" (2.1.289), and Cassio's "daily beauty" (5.1.19). He aspires to Cassio's job and Othello's "content" and tries to identify with their love for Desdemona—"now I do love her too" (2.1.286), although this love is immediately subsumed under notions of lust and revenge. The tension between his theoretical misogyny and his awareness of Desdemona's particular virtue drives him to resolve the conflicts, to turn that virtue "into pitch" (2.3.351), just as his verses extravagantly praise the deserving woman the better to be able to diminish her. Othello's conflict has the opposite issue; he murders Desdemona to redeem her from degradation.

The women in *Othello* are not murderous, nor are they foolishly idealistic or anxiously cynical, as the men are. From the start they, like the comedy heroines, combine realism with romance, mockery with affection. Bianca comically reflects the qualities of the women as Roderigo does those of the men. The play associates her with the other two women by means of the overheard conversation about her which Othello takes to be about Desdemona and by means of her irate and essentially just response to Emilia's attack: "I am no strumpet, but of life as honest / As you, that thus abuse me" (5.1.120–21). At this point, Iago tries to fabricate evidence against her, just as Othello, in the scene immediately following, fabricates a case against Desdemona. Bianca's active, open-eyed enduring affection is similar to that of the other women. She neither romanticizes love nor degrades sex. She sees Cassio's callousness but accepts it wryly—"'Tis very good, I must be circumstanc'd" (3.4.199). She mocks him to his face but not behind his back, as he does her. Her active pursuit of Cassio is in contrast to his indifference, to Roderigo's passivity, and to Othello's naiveté. Even when jealous, she continues to feel affection for Cassio, accusing him openly and demanding that he come to dinner on her terms. The play's humanization of her, much like, for example, that of the bourgeois characters at the end of *Love's Labor's Lost,* underlines the folly of the male characters (and critics) who see her as merely a whore.

Emilia articulates the balanced view that Bianca embodies—"and though we have some grace, / Yet have we some revenge" (4.3.92–93). She, like other Shakespearean shrews, especially Beatrice and Paulina, combines sharp-tongued honesty with warm affection. Her views are midway between Desdemona's and Bianca's and between those of the women and those of the men. She rejects the identification with Bianca yet sympathizes with female promiscuity. She corrects Desdemona's occasional naiveté but defends her chastity. Although she comprehends male jealousy and espouses sexual equality, she seems remarkably free from jealousy herself. She wittily sees cuckoldry and marital affection as compatible: "Who would not make her husband a cuckold, to make him a monarch?" (4.3.74–75). She understands, but tolerates, male fancy; the dangers of such tolerance become evident in this play as they never do in the comedies.

Desdemona's and Emilia's contrasting viewpoints in the willow scene have led critics to think of them as opposites, but both are strong, realistic, and compliant. When we first see them together, they encourage and participate in Iago's misogynist banter but reject his stereotypes. Desdemona here defends Emilia from Iago's insults just as Emilia will ultimately defend Desdemona from Othello's calumny. While Desdemona is no shrew (though she might be said to approach one in the matter of Cassio's reinstatement), her love is everywhere tempered by realism and wit like that of the comedy heroines. During courtship she hides, as they did, behind a sort of disguise, in this case not male dress, but a mask of docility and indifference which conceals her passion from both her father and Othello. Like Iago's docile and deserving woman she is one that could "think, and ne'er disclose her mind, / See suitors following, and not look behind" (2.1.156–57). Eventually, though, she takes the lead in the courtship as the heroines do; she finds an excuse to be alone with Othello, mocks him by speaking of him "dispraisingly" (3.3.73), and traps him into a proposal using indirection not unlike Rosalind's with Orlando.

After marriage, as during courtship, Desdemona's love tempers romance with realism, obedience with self-assertion. She is indifferent to Cassio's elaborate compliments (2.1.87ff.). She rejects Othello's desire to stop time, instead emphasizing love's growth. Her healthy, casual acceptance of sexuality is evident in her banter with Iago and with the clown, in her affirmation that she "did love the Moor, to live with him" (1.3.248), and in her refusal to postpone consummation of "the rites for which I love him" (1.3.257). She will not allow herself to be idealized; nor will she romanticize Othello. She had spoken "dispraisingly" of him during courtship, and she mocks him gently after marriage:

> Tell me, Othello: I wonder in my soul,
> What you could ask me, that I should deny?
> Or stand so mammering on?
>
> Shall I deny you? no, farewell, my lord.
>
> (3.3.69–71, 87)

She reminds herself, in an emphatically short line:

> nay, we must think
> Men are not gods;
> Nor of them look for such observances
> As fits the bridal.
>
> (3.4.145–48)

Her concise statement about her love reveals its balance and health:

> I saw Othello's visage in his mind,
> And to his honours, and his valiant parts
> Did I my soul and fortunes consecrate.
>
> (1.3.252–54)

She loves Othello for his body and mind, for his reputation and actions; she consecrates herself to him spiritually and practically.

Desdemona's spirit, clarity, and realism do not desert her entirely in the latter half of the play as many critics and performances imply. Her inability to defend herself is partly the result of Othello's refusal to voice his suspicions directly. When he does so in the brothel scene, she persistently questions him to discover exactly what he is accusing her of and defends herself as "stoutly" (3.1.45) as she had earlier defended Cassio: